This satiric book contains five lectures, two chapters (the first and the last) on the manufacture and consumption of something called tequila daisies in a rather special Tijuana bar, and a Foreword by Harold Benjamin. Professor Benjamin, who is thought to have had more than an editorial acquaintance with the contents of the chapters, is former Dean of the College of Education of the Universities of Colorado and Maryland, and Emeritus Professor of Education at the George Peabody College for Teachers. He has written a number of more or less imposing works, but he admits that Peddiwell's book of paleolithic essays is far more popular than any production of Harold Benjamin.

The Saber-Tooth Curriculum

SABER-TOOTH

. . . . *Including Other Lectures in the*

by J. ABNER PEDDIWELL, PH.D.
and SEVERAL TEQUILA DAISIES

McGRAW-HILL, INC.

CURRICULUM

History of Paleolithic Education . . . .

as told to RAYMOND WAYNE

with a Foreword by HAROLD BENJAMIN

NEW YORK AND LONDON

McGraw-Hill

A Division of The McGraw·Hill Companies

COPYRIGHT, 1939, BY THE
McGRAW-HILL BOOK COMPANY, INC.

PRINTED IN THE UNITED STATES OF AMERICA

41 42 43 44 45 46 47 48 49   BKM BKM   0 9 8 7 6 5 4 3 2 1

ISBN 07-049151-8

DEDICATION

*To the Two Young Professors Who Shared My Office
in the Summer of the Paper Famine*

DEAR COLLEAGUES:

Ordinarily a dedication is merely a gesture of affection.
In the present case, it is that and also an accusation of
being accessories before the fact, for I must charge you
with grave responsibility for the manner and substance
of these lectures. They were cast in narrative form to hold
your fickle attention; they avoid a definite tendency toward the educational left in deference to your youthful
conservatism; and they are brief because you borrowed
most of my paper.

Yours sincerely,

THE AUTHOR

FOREWORD

I HAVE read the following narrative and find it faintly amusing in spots. Perhaps there are even some theoretical suggestions of not wholly negligible significance beneath the fantastic and outlandish exterior.

I must raise several grave questions, however, concerning the professional standing, general reliability, and, to speak quite bluntly, the veracity of the author or authors. I have consulted various biographical directories and the membership lists of some of the most important educational organizations, and I fail to find any evidence whatever of the existence of a man named J. Abner Peddiwell. If there is a man of that name, I doubt that he is a professor of education. Furthermore, I have examined the most recent edition of the national directory of institutions of higher education, published by the United States Office of Education, and I am unable to discover any mention of the Petaluma State College of whose faculty the so-called Professor Peddiwell is allegedly a member.

It seems probable, therefore, that these *soisant-dit* lectures are solely the work of the flashily dressed young man who submitted the manuscript to me in person. My secretary granted him an interview with me under the impression that he was, at best, a sales representative of one of the college textbook publishing companies or, at worst, a life insurance salesman. He entered my office breezily, greeted me familiarly, said his name was Raymond Wayne, and claimed to have been one of my students some ten years ago.

When I asked this self-assured young man to leave an address to which I might forward my comments on the manuscript, he refused to do so on the following grounds: (1) the nature of his business was such that he had no permanent address, (2) he knew without any comments from me that the manuscript was good, and (3) he could learn of the publication of the book by reading laudatory reviews of it in professional journals.

Although the man's extreme assurance irritated me beyond ordinary measure, I controlled my resentment and asked him how it would be possible to send him his royalties in the event of the manuscript's publication and in the further event that anyone should buy the book after publication. He replied that he desired me to collect the royalties and use them for giving professors of education some basic training in methods of teaching.

"Do you expect the hypothetical royalties from this hypothetical publication to be large enough for such a noble purpose?" I asked sarcastically.

"Frankly, no," he replied. "It would take all the resources of the Carnegie Foundation for the Advancement of Teaching even to make a beginning on a job as big as that. But it's the principle of the thing I want to establish. You spend the first fifty thousand of my royalties on the project, and then maybe each of the big foundations will kick in a million or two apiece and we'll get somewhere."

This is probably an adequate sampling of the man's attitude toward the whole system of modern education. The more important question of his reliability may easily be checked against some of his specific statements.

The author claims in his introductory chapter that he is a member of Phi Beta Kappa and received the baccalaureate degree with great distinction. Although I cannot refute this statement by appeal to documents, I must insist that indirect evidence from the manuscript itself leads to the inescapable conclusion that the person who wrote it possessed neither the coveted key nor the arts degree *magna cum laude*. The contempt displayed by the author for many of the basic principles underlying the academic processes leading to these distinctions is in itself sufficient to stamp him as one whose own education, on the liberal side at least, was sadly neglected. In fact it is difficult to resist the suspicion that the man who wrote the following pages does not believe that the great cultural verities are eternal, changeless, possessing a certain indefinable and imponderable something whose essence is timelessness.

In conclusion, therefore, I submit this work with the following summary of my judgments concerning the authorship claimed on the title page.

There is no professor of education named J. Abner Peddiwell.

The man who calls himself Raymond Wayne is probably antagonistic to liberal culture and is almost certainly a liar.

The "Several Tequila Daisies" mentioned as coauthors of this narrative apparently involve the alcoholic phase of the presentation, comment on which is beneath my contempt.

Harold Benjamin.

CONTENTS

xiii

THE SABER-TOOTH CURRICULUM

I · SEMINAR IN TIJUANA

THE longest bar in the world, as I suppose almost everybody knows, is in Tijuana. It is on the left side of the main street just after you cross the border looking for relaxation. If you stand at the middle of that bar and look to right and left long enough with a pair of field glasses, you will eventually see everyone in the world who believes that tequila daisies and relaxation go together. Of course, you would never expect to find there a man who was ignorant of both terms in that famous pair of remedies for mental and spiritual malaise, yet that is what happened to me when I had my last near approach to a nervous breakdown and was easily persuaded

3

to take a two weeks' vacation south of the border.

It was my first day in Tijuana. I had just ordered one more tequila daisy and was gazing at the starboard wing of the bar with what seemed to be a clear and untroubled vision when I saw a sober brown suit on a compact but rotund figure approach the bar about fifty meters from where I was stationed. A decade earlier, during my upper division work at the Petaluma State College, that suit and the personality which gave it meaning and character had been hammered into my consciousness five hours a week, forty weeks a year, until my response to them was automatic.

At first I stared in disbelief. My reason told me that this phenomenon could not be in Tijuana; that, most of all, it was impossible in a place selling liquor. Despite the evidence of my eyes and memory, it seemed certain that what I was experiencing was merely an illusion occasioned by the impact of tequila daisies on deeply carved neural pathways.

"Luis," I called, "how many daisies have I had?"

"Eet ees onlee your fort' wan," the bartender answered, a little reproachfully, as though it was hardly yet time for me to become talkative.

I looked again, and there the illusion still stood, leaning against the bar, waiting for service.

"Do you see a short, fattish bird in a funny looking brown suit up the bar there a ways?" I asked.

Luis looked and nodded. "Beer," he diagnosed sadly, "joos' to say he ees dreenk at de longes' bar een de worl'."

"Beer!" I repeated. "Never! Not a drop of alcohol in any form if that man is who I think he is. Beat it up there, Luis, and get his order. Quick!"

Luis obeyed slowly, mumbling as he went, "Alcohol, hell! Beer ees joos' beer."

The four tequila daisies could not have been enough to blur or otherwise distort my vision. It must have been an excess of emotion that caused me momentarily to lose sight of Luis and the customer in the brown suit. I waited, supporting my body against the bar, my heart pounding in my throat. If by some miracle the impossible had happened and the hero of my university days was really in this place, I knew that I should have to pay my respects, even though running the risk of having tequila smelled on my breath.

At length Luis's face, steered by its long mustaches, loomed again through the fog across the bar.

"What did he order?" I demanded hoarsely.

"Notheeng," replied Luis disgustedly. "He joos' weesh to know how een hell we are sure dees ees longes' bar een de worl'. W'ere een hell ees our proof, he say."

"Did he—did he actually say *hell?*" I asked almost in a whisper.

"Oh, no. *I* am say *hell*. De professor, he speak deeferent, but w'at he wan' to know ees how een hell we—"

"*Professor?* Did he say he was a professor?"

"Sure—he claim he ees professor een Petaluma Colegio, an' he wan' to know how een hell—"

Luis's voice faded into a receding monotone while I straightened my necktie, pulled down my vest, and set my hat in square respectability. The miracle had happened. I would have paid my

"If you ask me to prove that it is the longest bar in the world, I shall ask you to prove that it is not the longest."

respects, if necessary, through a barrier of forty tequila daisies. The pleasant, warm mist of a trifling four could not deter me for a moment.

"Dr. Peddiwell," I began as I approached the great scholar, who was still waiting for evidence to support the bar's claim of dimensional superiority.

He turned and touched his hat with characteristic courtesy. "Your face is familiar," he said automatically, "but I am afraid I—"

"Wayne—Raymond Wayne," I supplied, removing my hat. "You won't remember me, Doctor, but I was in your classes at Petaluma ten years ago, and I—"

"Of course, *of course!*" He shook my hand warmly. "Your name, sir, was right on the tip of my tongue. Remember you? Why certainly I remember you. An *A* student, you were, if my memory does not play me false."

"Yes, sir, and Phi Beta Kappa," I murmured modestly.

"Of course, of *course.*"

"A. B., *magna cum laude,*" I continued.

"Certainly, of *course.*"

8

"Major in history of education."

"Well, well! My own field! Of course I remember you, Mr.—Mr.—"

"Wayne—Raymond Wayne."

"Mr. Wayne, of *course*. And where are you teaching now?"

"Well, Doctor, I—er—I am not—er—teaching anywhere at present."

"Not teaching? That's terrible! Major in History of Education—*A* student—everything. We must find a teaching position for you at once."

"Well—I haven't been looking for a teaching position for several years."

"You haven't? But—what are you—what is your—?"

"I—I am selling electric washing machines."

"A traveling salesman?"

"Well, in a certain way, yes."

"Of *course*, many advantages in that line of endeavor, I can see at once."

"A few, yes, sir—money, for instance."

"Er—quite so—and travel—you see a good many towns and cities in your journeys about the country, do you not?"

9

"Well, some, yes."

"And these—er—bars also?"

"Why—sometimes—yes. You know, Doctor—entertaining prospects, having sales conferences—that sort of thing."

"Ah, yes. And is it your judgment, on the basis of your observations, that this is actually the longest bar in the world?"

"It's the longest one *I* ever saw, Doctor."

"Excuse my insistence, but have you ever measured it?"

"Well—er—no."

"Have you ever measured any other bar?"

"Why, no, I don't believe I ever have."

"Ah, then—forgive any semblance of cross-examination—how do you *know* that this is the longest bar in the world?" He paused pityingly. Then, without waiting for an answer, wishing in his kindly way to spare me further embarrassment, he hastened on, "I shall not press the point to a tiresome length, but you grasp the issue, Mr.—Mr.—?"

"Wayne," I supplied automatically, grateful for being permitted once more to see that flawless intellect in operation.

"Of *course*, Mr. Wayne. You took my course in History of the Science of Education, did you not?"

"Yes, sir, I took *all* your courses."

"You will perhaps remember my lecture on the testing of hypotheses?"

"Doctor, I remember *all* your lectures."

"Thank you, sir. You recall the central proposition in that lecture?"

"Well—er—I . . . "

"Briefly stated, it ran to the general effect that education becomes scientific in proportion to the increasing willingness of educationists to test their hypotheses."

"Yes, sir."

"Very well. The hypothesis concerning the length of this bar offers an interesting example. Here we have hundreds of tourists daily, perhaps, all of whom are told and many of whom believe that this is the longest bar in the world. These tourists are being educated through the medium of an hypothesis, an untested hypothesis, an hypothesis unsupported by objective evidence, an hypothesis naked of precise data In this regard, therefore, the curriculum for these tourists is medieval. It is a faith-conjecture-guess curriculum built on a maximum of speculation and a minimum of exact observation. What is needed in the Tijuana-tourist educational system, as in other more formal systems all over the world, is an increase in careful measurement, and a decrease in fantastic humbug!"

Peddiwell liked critical ability in his students, so I was ready with an argument as soon as he paused.

"With your main proposition," I said, "there can be no quarrel. The testing of hypotheses is an ultimate necessity in any science. It seems possible, however, that you are minimizing the importance of the initial hypothesis. We need some fantastic conjectures at first in order later to have anything to test. We must first be subjective in a large way in order that we may afterward become objective in the grand manner. We should not forget that the wildest hypothesis may conceivably serve a useful scientific purpose more effectively than a hundred researchers working with objective scores from a thousand tests, aided by ten thousand statisticians with a hundred thousand calculating machines, grinding out a million correlations, ten million probable errors, a hundred million indexes of the significance of differences, a billion—"

I hesitated, becoming suddenly aware that the professor was looking at me curiously and that the figures I was quoting, as well as the pitch of my voice, both of them a trifle stepped up by four daisies, were becoming somewhat extravagant.

"Take the hypothesis concerning the length of this bar," I continued in a more moderate tone. "Here we have a specific instance of an untested generalization with great potential utility. You neglect, for example, the potentially important social purpose served by this hypothesis."

"Indeed!" He raised his eyebrows. "May I ask what useful purpose could possibly be served by an hypothesis relating to grandiose claims to bigness of an agency devoted to the dispensing of alcoholic liquors?"

By this time I could see quite clearly that the tequila I had slapped rather hurriedly on a relatively empty stomach was beginning to accelerate my mental processes and lower the threshold of my inhibitions. My formally educated cerebrum noted this fact and counseled caution, but my daisy-educated, subcortical self gave an inner whoop of delight and tossed caution overboard.

"The integration of the human personality, Doctor, that's the answer," I said.

The great man stared at me coldly. "It is a well-known fact, sir," he began, "that alcohol, even when consumed in minute quantities, has depressive if not actually deleterious effects on the—"

The daisies got behind me and pushed me into an interruption. "Physiologically," I announced, "only physiologically, and then only when we define the term in a narrow and non-organismic way. With a minor physiological effect, however, we are not concerned. We are students of behavior-modifying goals, agencies, instruments, procedures. We are educationists, which is to say applied psychologists. We work with men—men in action—men in action directed towards the betterment of their lives!"

The professor expelled air violently through the nose. "Humph! Those verbalizations may be all right for an introductory course, but here and now I want something specific."

"All right, Doctor, here's an instance. Consider the case of a downtrodden tourist—a traveling Joe Doakes from Podunkville—a man accustomed in his usual habitat to being small potatoes, browbeaten by a domineering boss and snapped into line by a strong-willed wife, a man who gets his political opinions from Mr. Hearst's hireling pundits and his economic views from Colonel McCormick, a man who is perforce satisfied to live in a small place, work at a small job, and occupy an inferior status in general."

"A sad picture," observed the professor sympathetically, "and one which in certain respects fits many a man whom the world regards as occupying an important position and holding superior status. I have known a Governor Joe Doakes, several Captain Doakeses, and in the academic world, sir, the name of Doakes might well be borne even by certain deans and presidents."

"Exactly, Doctor, but consider the case of this hypothetical little man a trifle further. Everything in his existence combines to make him feel unimportant. His personality becomes disintegrated. And *then*, Doctor, this individual is enabled to come to Tijuana for a vacation. He is able to come alone, without his wife or other representative of authority. He comes into this barroom and—"

"Of course, of *course*," interrupted the professor briskly. "I see—no wife—no boss—freedom—personality expands and integrates—but—"

"He comes into this barroom," I continued hurriedly, "and at once the management does the socially valuable thing. It tells him he is in a unique place, not uniquely unimportant like himself, but uniquely great as he does not dare to dream of being. Under the impact of this suggestion his personality begins to unfold and blossom like a drought-withered flower under a cooling, gentle rain."

"Yes, yes," said the professor approvingly. "Quite neatly, even artistically, put, but you cannot gainsay the damning fact that this place is devoted to the sale of alcohol, and your pathetic little man will be tempted to—"

"Quite so, and that is a part of the treatment. The barroom suggests to our little, unimportant hero that he can become a part of this uniquely great phenomenon by drinking at the bar. Therefore, he drinks—maybe beer, in which case his personality becomes a trifle better integrated; maybe wine, which helps his personality somewhat more; maybe hard liquor, like whiskey or rum, whereupon he may become markedly integrated; or maybe, if he is fortunate, tequila in the form known as the tequila daisy, which expands his personality in a uniquely effective manner."

"And—er—what is tequila?"

"It is a distilled liquor, a spirit—spirit is a good word—it is the liquid soul of certain varieties of the *maguey·* plant. Among the derivatives of *maguey*, tequila stands supreme as an integrator of the human personality."

Up to that moment I had assumed that the discussion was purely academic. You will understand my astonishment, therefore, at the professor's next move. Deliberately he stepped away from the bar and regarded himself at one of the image-distorting mirrors along the back wall. Slowly he loosened his necktie. With a kind of precise carelessness he unbuttoned the coat of that famous brown suit. With obvious satisfaction he looked at the abnormally elongated and slender figure which the trick mirror gave him. Gravely he turned to where I stood waiting.

"If you don't mind," he announced, "I will have one of these tequila daisies."

A fear clutched my throat, a fear that I might faint before I could give the order for the drink, a fear that I might thus miss seeing the first contact between two great spirits. But some measure of the courage of my fighting ancestors carried me through. I called Luis and ordered two tequila daisies.

"My wife," remarked Dr. Peddiwell at the end of his first daisy, "is in San Diego, Mr.—er—"

"Wayne," I said, recalling the image of a most determined-looking woman who had seemed to dislike me thoroughly whenever she had seen me in her husband's seminar.

"Of *course*. Yes, sir, my wife is attending a national convention of the League of American Needlewomen. She is an official delegate from the Petaluma chapter or local of that organization.

Indeed, if my memory does not play me false, she is chairman of the state committee on the relationship between economic planning and cross-stitching."

"Ah, very interesting," I commented politely, "and—er—exciting, too, for Mrs. Peddiwell, no doubt, and—ah—probably quite useful as well— needle craft and all that sort of thing." I labored heavily, wishing that the professor would not dwell on the activities of that woman. I did not care whether she was in San Diego or in a locality reputed to have a much less comfortable climate. With five daisies under my belt, moreover, I hated to pretend that I did care.

"And do you know where *I* am at the present time?" pursued the professor.

"In Tijuana, Baja California, Republica Mexicana," I replied promptly, the daisies giving me a good Castilian accent.

"In a certain objective and geographically tested sense, yes," agreed Peddiwell, "but in a more hypothetical and maritally correct sense, no. So far as Mrs. Peddiwell is concerned, I am at this moment and for the rest of the week in the library of the University of California at Berkeley engaged in scholarly labors."

I looked at the man with a new respect. My old adolescent admiration for him was enriched and enhanced by a mature delight in the unsuspected depths of his character. A man who could lie so completely to that lantern-jawed Mrs. Peddiwell and get away with it was one whom I could follow to hell through a great forest of tequila daisies. I had an impulse to climb upon the bar and declaim his praises, but I inhibited this reaction as being undignified and was just about to indicate to the bartender that our glasses were empty when Dr. Peddiwell anticipated me.

"Luis," he called, slapping the bar with his open hand in a most emphatic manner, "two more daisies—and kindly snap out of your dope!"

At the end of the second round, the professor's usual fleeting and delicate smile had assumed a certain degree of careless permanency and robustness. He set down his glass and regarded me benignly. "I wish to say frankly," he stated in full lecture-room voice, "that I now appreciate your point of view concerning the social value of certain fantastic and unsupported hypotheses. May I ask whether you have considerable time to spend in this place?"

"Two weeks, Doctor."

"Good, I have five days. The time is adequate though not excessive. The student body is well educated in the fundamentals—one hundred per cent Phi Beta Kappa. The lecture room is the longest of its kind in the world. If you ask me to prove that it is the longest, I shall ask you to prove that it is not the longest. The instructor is, I hope, not altogether unprepared. Under these circumstances, I propose a seminar—in the history of paleolithic education—hypothetical, fantastic, conjectural—lectures and discussion—no term reports or—Luis! *Que hombre!* Don't you see these empty glasses?"

At the end of the doctor's third daisy, which you must remember was the seventh one for me, I confess that my own frame of reference was becoming a bit unreal. I could catch only a sentence or two as they came dancing by in gay circles.

"Mr.—er—your confounded name seems to elude me," observed the professor, wiping a daisy drop off his lapel, "that is to say, your surname eludes me. What is your Christian name?"

"Chris'—Chris'n name?"

"Yes, your first name, you know."

"Oh! Firs' name? Firs' name's Ray—Raymon'."

"Raymond? Ah, hell! That is more difficult to remember than your last name! Hereafter, with your permission, I shall call you Bill—or Pete."

"'S'all ri' with me, old-timer," I assured him. "Don' give a double-edge' damn what you call me jus' so long's you lecture on hist'ry of pale—pal—lithya—*that* kind of education."

"I'll start tomorrow," he told me, "when my class is somewhat more on its intellectual toes, as it were."

I do not know whether we had any more daisies on that occasion. A careful search of my memory for the remainder of the evening yields only two fragments. One of them glimpses Dr. Peddiwell hailing a passing schoolma'am tourist from the United States as "Bright eyes"; the other reveals him singing lullabies to me in a taxicab on our way to the hotel in Agua Caliente—at least the tunes were reminiscent of lullabies, although the words appeared to be derived in part from the professor's early experiences as a whistle-pup in an Oregon logging camp.

II · THE SABER-TOOTH CURRICULUM

THE first great educational theorist and practitioner of whom my imagination has any record (began Dr. Peddiwell in his best professorial tone) was a man of Chellean times whose full name was *New-Fist-Hammer-Maker* but whom, for convenience, I shall hereafter call *New-Fist*.

New-Fist was a doer, in spite of the fact that there was little in his environment with which to do anything very complex. You have undoubtedly heard of the pear-shaped, chipped-stone tool which archeologists call the *coup-de-poing* or fist hammer. New-Fist gained his name and a considerable local prestige by producing one of these artifacts in a less rough and more useful form than any previously known to his tribe. His hunting clubs were generally superior weapons, moreover, and his fire-using techniques were patterns of simplicity and precision. He knew how to do things his community needed to have done, and he had the energy and will to go ahead and do them. By virtue of these characteristics he was an educated man.

New-Fist was also a thinker. Then, as now, there were few lengths to which men would not go to avoid the labor and pain of thought. More readily than his fellows, New-Fist pushed himself beyond those lengths to the point where cerebration was inevitable. The same quality of intelligence which led him into the socially approved activity of producing a superior artifact also led him to engage in the socially disapproved practice of thinking. When other men gorged themselves on the proceeds of a successful hunt and vegetated in dull stupor for many hours thereafter, New-Fist ate a little less heartily, slept a little less stupidly, and arose a little earlier than his comrades to sit by the fire and think. He would stare moodily at the flickering flames and wonder about various parts of his environment until he finally got to the point where he became strongly dissatisfied with the accustomed ways of his tribe. He began to catch glimpses of ways in which life might be made better for himself, his family, and his group. By virtue of this development, he became a dangerous man.

This was the background that made this doer and thinker hit upon the concept of a conscious, systematic education. The immediate stimulus which put him directly into the practice of education came from watching his children at play. He saw these children at the cave entrance before the fire engaged in activity with bones and sticks and brightly colored pebbles. He noted that they seemed to have no purpose in their play beyond immediate pleasure in the activity itself. He compared their activity with that of the grown-up members of the tribe. The children played for fun the adults worked for security and enrichment of their lives. The children dealt with bones, sticks, and pebbles; the adults dealt with food, shelter, and clothing. The children protected themselves

"They are living what they learn, and learning what they live."

27

from boredom; the adults protected themselves from danger.

"If I could only get these children to do the things that will give more and better food, shelter, clothing, and security," thought New-Fist, "I would be helping this tribe to have a better life. When the children became grown, they would have more meat to eat, more skins to keep them warm, better caves in which to sleep, and less danger from the striped death with the curving teeth that walks these trails by night."

Having set up an educational goal, New-Fist proceeded to construct a curriculum for reaching that goal. "What things must we tribesmen know how to do in order to live with full bellies, warm backs, and minds free from fear?" he asked himself.

To answer this question, he ran various activities over in his mind. "We have to catch fish with our bare hands in the pool far up the creek beyond that big bend," he said to himself. "We have to catch fish with our bare hands in the pool right at the bend. We have to catch them in the same way in the pool just this side of the bend. And so we catch them in the next pool and the next and the next. Always we catch them with our bare hands."

Thus New-Fist discovered the first subject of the first curriculum—fish-grabbing-with-the-bare-hands.

"Also we club the little woolly horses," he continued with his analysis. "We club them along the bank of the creek where they come down to drink. We club them in the thickets where they lie down to sleep. We club them in the upland meadow where they graze. Wherever we find them we club them."

So woolly-horse-clubbing was seen to be the second main subject in the curriculum.

"And finally, we drive away the saber-tooth tigers with fire," New-Fist went on in his thinking. "We drive them from the mouth of our caves with fire. We drive them from our trail with burning branches. We wave firebrands to drive them from our drinking hole. Always we have to drive them away, and always we drive them with fire."

Thus was discovered the third subject—saber-tooth-tiger-scaring-with-fire.

Having developed a curriculum, New-Fist took his children with him as he went about his activities. He gave them an opportunity to practice these three subjects. The children liked to learn. It was more fun for them to engage in these purposeful activities than to play with colored stones just for the fun of it. They learned the new activities well, and so the educational system was a success.

As New-Fist's children grew older, it was plain to see that they had an advantage in good and safe living over other children who had never been educated systematically. Some of the more intelligent members of the tribe began to do as New-Fist had done, and the teaching of fish-grabbing, horse-clubbing, and tiger-scaring came more and more to be accepted as the heart of real education.

For a long time, however, there were certain more conservative members of the tribe who resisted the new, formal educational system on religious grounds. "The Great Mystery who speaks in thunder and moves in lightning," they announced impressively, "the Great Mystery who gives men life and takes it from them as he wills—

if that Great Mystery had wanted children to practice fish-grabbing, horse-clubbing, and tiger-scaring before they were grown up, he would have taught them these activities himself by implanting in their natures instincts for fish-grabbing, horse-clubbing, and tiger-scaring. New-Fist is not only impious to attempt something the Great Mystery never intended to have done; he is also a damned fool for trying to change human nature."

Whereupon approximately half of these critics took up the solemn chant, "If you oppose the will of the Great Mystery, you must die," and the remainder sang derisively in unison, "You can't change human nature."

Being an educational statesman as well as an educational administrator and theorist, New-Fist replied politely to both arguments. To the more theologically minded, he said that, as a matter of fact, the Great Mystery had ordered this new work done, that he even did the work himself by causing children to want to learn, that children could not learn by themselves without divine aid, that they could not learn at all except through the power of the Great Mystery, and that nobody could really understand the will of the Great Mystery concerning fish, horses, and saber-tooth tigers unless he had been well grounded in the three fundamental subjects of the New-Fist school. To the human-nature-cannot-be-changed shouters, New-Fist pointed out the fact that paleolithic culture had attained its high level by changes in human nature and that it seemed almost unpatriotic to deny the very process which had made the community great.

"I know you, my fellow tribesmen," the pioneer educator ended his argument gravely, "I know you as humble and devoted servants of the Great Mystery. I know that you would not for one moment consciously oppose yourselves to his will. I know you as intelligent and loyal citizens of this great cave-realm, and I know that your pure and noble patriotism will not permit you to do anything which will block the development of that most cave-realmish of all our institutions—the paleolithic educational system. Now that you understand the true nature and purpose of this institution, I am serenely confident that there are no reasonable lengths to which you will not go in its defense and its support."

By this appeal the forces of conservatism were won over to the side of the new school, and in due time everybody who was anybody in the community knew that the heart of good education lay in the three subjects of fish-grabbing, horse-clubbing, and tiger-scaring. New-Fist and his contemporaries grew old and were gathered by the Great Mystery to the Land of the Sunset far down the creek. Other men followed their educational ways more and more, until at last all the children of the tribe were practiced systematically in the three fundamentals. Thus the tribe prospered and was happy in the possession of adequate meat, skins, and security.

It is to be supposed that all would have gone well forever with this good educational system if conditions of life in that community had remained forever the same. But conditions changed, and life which had once been so safe and happy in the cave-realm valley became insecure and disturbing.

A new ice age was approaching in that part of the world. A great glacier came down from the neighboring mountain range to the north. Year after year it crept closer and closer to the head-waters of the creek which ran through the tribe's valley, until at length it reached the stream and began to melt into the water. Dirt and gravel which the glacier had collected on its long journey were dropped into the creek. The water grew muddy. What had once been a crystal-clear stream in which one could see easily to the bottom was now a milky stream into which one could not see at all.

At once the life of the community was changed in one very important respect. It was no longer possible to catch fish with the bare hands. The fish could not be seen in the muddy water. For some years, moreover, the fish in this creek had been getting more timid, agile, and intelligent. The stupid, clumsy, brave fish, of which originally there had been a great many, had been caught with the bare hands for fish generation after fish genera-tion, until only fish of superior intelligence and agility were left. These smart fish, hiding in the muddy water under the newly deposited glacial boulders, eluded the hands of the most expertly trained fish-grabbers. Those tribesmen who had studied advanced fish-grabbing in the secondary school could do no better than their less well-educated fellows who had taken only an elementary course in the subject, and even the university graduates with majors in ichthyology were baffled by the problem. No matter how good a man's fish-grabbing education had been, he could not grab fish when he could not find fish to grab.

The melting waters of the approaching ice sheet also made the country wetter. The ground became marshy far back from the banks of the creek. The stupid woolly horses, standing only five or six hands high and running on four-toed front feet and three-toed hind feet, although admirable objects for clubbing, had one dangerous characteristic. They were ambitious. They all wanted to learn to run on their middle toes. They all had visions of becoming powerful and aggressive animals instead of little and timid ones. They dreamed of a far-distant day when some of their descendants would be sixteen hands high, weigh more than half a ton, and be able to pitch their would-be riders into the dirt. They knew they could never attain these goals in a wet, marshy country, so they all went east to the dry, open plains, far from the paleolithic hunting grounds. Their places were taken by little antelopes who came down with the ice sheet and were so shy and speedy and had so keen a scent for danger that no one could approach them closely enough to club them.

The best trained horse-clubbers of the tribe went out day after day and employed the most efficient techniques taught in the schools, but day after day they returned empty-handed. A horse-clubbing education of the highest type could get no results when there were no horses to club

Finally, to complete the disruption of paleolithic life and education, the new dampness in the air gave the saber-tooth tigers pneumonia, a disease to which these animals were peculiarly susceptible and to which most of them succumbed. A few moth-eaten specimens crept south to the desert, it is true, but they were pitifully few and weak representatives of a once numerous and powerful race.

So there were no more tigers to scare in the paleolithic community, and the best tiger-scaring techniques became only academic exercises, good in themselves, perhaps, but not necessary for tribal security. Yet this danger to the people was lost only to be replaced by another and even greater danger, for with the advancing ice sheet came ferocious glacial bears which were not afraid of fire, which walked the trails by day as well as by night, and which could not be driven away by the most advanced methods developed in the tiger-scaring courses of the schools.

The community was now in a very difficult situation. There was no fish or meat for food, no hides for clothing, and no security from the hairy death that walked the trails day and night. Adjustment to this difficulty had to be made at once if the tribe was not to become extinct.

Fortunately for the tribe, however, there were men in it of the old New-Fist breed, men who had the ability to do and the daring to think. One of them stood by the muddy stream, his stomach contracting with hunger pains, longing for some way to get a fish to eat. Again and again he had tried the old fish-grabbing technique that day, hoping desperately that at last it might work, but now in black despair he finally rejected all that he had learned in the schools and looked about him for some new way to get fish from that stream. There were stout but slender vines hanging from trees along the bank. He pulled them down and began to fasten them together more or less aimlessly. As he worked, the vision of what he might do to satisfy his hunger and that of his crying children back in the cave grew clearer. His black despair lightened a little. He worked more rapidly and intelligently. At last he had it—a net, a crude seine. He called a companion and explained the device. The two men took the net into the water, into pool after pool, and in one hour they caught more fish—intelligent fish in muddy water—than the whole tribe could have caught in a day under the best fish-grabbing conditions.

Another intelligent member of the tribe wandered hungrily through the woods where once the stupid little horses had abounded but where now only the elusive antelope could be seen. He had tried the horse-clubbing technique on the antelope until he was fully convinced of its futility. He knew that one would starve who relied on school learning to get him meat in those woods. Thus it was that he too, like the fish-net inventor, was finally impelled by hunger to new ways. He bent a strong, springy young tree over an antelope trail, hung a noosed vine therefrom, and fastened the whole device in so ingenious a fashion that the passing animal would release a trigger and be snared neatly when the tree jerked upright. By setting a line of these snares, he was able in one night to secure more meat and skins than a dozen horse-clubbers in the old days had secured in a week.

A third tribesman, determined to meet the problem of the ferocious bears, also forgot what he had been taught in school and began to think in direct and radical fashion. Finally, as a result of this thinking, he dug a deep pit in a bear trail, covered it with branches in such a way that a bear would walk out on it unsuspectingly, fall through to the bottom, and remain trapped until the tribesmen could come up and despatch him with sticks and stones at their leisure. The inventor showed his friends how to dig and camouflage other pits until all the trails around the community were furnished with them. Thus the tribe had even more security than before and in addition had the great additional store of meat and skins which they secured from the captured bears.

As the knowledge of these new inventions spread, all the members of the tribe were engaged in familiarizing themselves with the new ways of living. Men worked hard at making fish nets, setting antelope snares, and digging bear pits. The tribe was busy and prosperous.

There were a few thoughtful men who asked questions as they worked. Some of them even criticized the schools.

"These new activities of net-making and operating, snare-setting, and pit-digging are indispensable to modern existence," they said. "Why can't they be taught in school?"

The safe and sober majority had a quick reply to this naïve question. "School!" they snorted derisively. "You aren't in school now. You are out here in the dirt working to preserve the life and happiness of the tribe. What have these practical activities got to do with schools? You're not saying lessons now. You'd better forget your lessons and your academic ideals of fish-grabbing, horse-clubbing, and tiger-scaring if you want to eat, keep warm, and have some measure of security from sudden death."

The radicals persisted a little in their questioning. "Fishnet-making and using, antelope-snare construction and operation, and bear-catching and killing," they pointed out, "require intelligence and skills—things we claim to develop in schools. They are also activities we need to know. Why can't the schools teach them?"

But most of the tribe, and particularly the wise old men who controlled the school, smiled indulgently at this suggestion. "That wouldn't be *education*," they said gently.

"But why wouldn't it be?" asked the radicals.

"Because it would be mere training," explained the old men patiently. "With all the intricate details of fish-grabbing, horse-clubbing, and tiger-scaring—the standard cultural subjects—the school curriculum is too crowded now. We can't add these fads and frills of net-making, antelope-snaring, and—of all things—bear-killing. Why, at the very thought, the body of the great New-Fist, founder of our paleolithic educational system, would turn over in its burial cairn. What we need to do is to give our young people a more thorough grounding in the fundamentals. Even the graduates of the secondary schools don't know the art of fish-grabbing in any complete sense nowadays, they swing their horse clubs awkwardly too, and as for the old science of tiger-scaring—well, even the teachers seem to lack the real flair for the subject which we oldsters got in our teens and never forgot."

"But, damn it," exploded one of the radicals, "how can any person with good sense be interested in such useless activities? What is the point of trying to catch fish with the bare hands when it just can't be done any more. How can a boy learn to club horses when there are no horses left to club? And why in hell should children try to scare tigers with fire when the tigers are dead and gone?"

"Don't be foolish," said the wise old men, smiling most kindly smiles. "We don't teach fish-grabbing to grab fish; we teach it to develop a generalized agility which can never be developed by mere training. We don't teach horse-clubbing to club horses; we teach it to develop a generalized strength in the learner which he can never get from so prosaic and specialized a thing as antelope-snare-setting. We don't teach tiger-scaring to scare tigers; we teach it for the purpose of giving that noble courage which carries over into all the affairs of life and which can never come from so base an activity as bear-killing."

All the radicals were silenced by this statement, all except the one who was most radical of all. He felt abashed, it is true, but he was so radical that he made one last protest.

"But—but anyway," he suggested, "you will have to admit that times have changed. Couldn't you please *try* these other more up-to-date activities? Maybe they have *some* educational value after all?"

Even the man's fellow radicals felt that this was going a little too far.

The wise old men were indignant. Their kindly smiles faded. "If you had any education yourself," they said severely, "you would know that the essence of true education is timelessness. It is something that endures through changing conditions like a solid rock standing squarely and firmly in the middle of a raging torrent. You must know that there are some eternal verities, and the saber-tooth curriculum is one of them!"

III · THE REAL-TIGER SCHOOL

 "THOSE trick mirrors are good," I remarked idly as Dr. Peddiwell and I leaned against the bar rail and surveyed the glittering frames along the wall.

"They distort life," the professor commented judicially.

"But they are funny, and they help to enliven the general *Gestalt* of this place," I pointed out.

"Ah, yes, but they are unreal, artificial," he insisted. "They do not teach us to learn what we live and live what we learn. They have no proper function in a progressive educational institution like this lecture room."

"I didn't know you were a progressive educationist," I murmured.

"Well, in one way I am, in another I am not," he replied cautiously.

"What do you mean?" I pressed, knowing that he was on the verge of a lecture. "There is only one kind of progressive education, isn't there?"

"You would not ask so naïve a question, were it not for your lack of historical perspective." His voice took on the accustomed intonation of a first paragraph. "Any careful student of the history of education can tell you that there were progressives and progressives in the past and that the best prediction indicates there will be progressives and progressives in the future. Progressives with new purposes and old machines, progressives with new machines and old purposes, progressives with old machines *and* purposes plus a few new verbalizations to make them less forlorn, and others— others—"

He left his sentence suspended in mid-air and stood gazing at a mirror which magnified his plumpness enormously.

"Was there any progressive education in paleolithic times?" I prompted.

"There was the Real-Tiger School, of course," he said absently, still staring at the mirror, "and also—er—the School of Creative Fish-Grabbing. You remember the quarrel that raged between these two progressive institutions, however, and consequently I do not need to—"

"But I *don't* remember," I interrupted. "You never told me."

He tore his gaze from the fat reflection and recovered his usual briskness. "Very good. We are then justified in devoting at least one period to that particular chain of events."

I settled myself and waited for the lecture.

After the new fishnet era was well under way (Dr. Peddiwell began) there was marked dissatisfaction with the traditional school. This dissatisfaction was really directed towards the teachers, for in those days the patrons of the school had the notion that a particular curriculum was really a certain kind of teacher, that a particular system of methods was a certain kind of teacher, and that the whole philosophy of the school was also just a certain kind of teacher. It was a peculiar notion, I admit—unbelievably simple, and all that—but the people had it. Of course they were courteous enough not to *say*, in most cases, that it was the teacher who was at fault. They talked about a better educational philosophy, an improved organization, and all that sort of thing very much as we do today.

By the beginning of the fishnet era, the profession of teaching was pretty well developed, and after the era was well under way, the status and preparation of teachers were rather adequately standardized. In the earlier days of the real-tiger era, teachers had been largely recruited from the ranks of those tribesmen who were too clumsy to grab fish, too weak to club horses, or too timid to face a saber-tooth. By the middle of the fishnet era, this situation had been vastly improved. Teachers were still selected to some extent from the more stupid and less aggressive elements of the population, but any slight disadvantage arising from that condition was more than offset by the new requirements for possession of the teacher's bone.

"To learn tiger-scaring, it is quite helpful to have a real tiger."

The chiefs of the tribe were the ones who made the rules in this regard as they did in any other matters affecting the peace, prosperity, security, and happiness of the people. According to these rules, every teacher had to carry with him at all times an official bone, usually the thigh bone of an antelope, upon which was scratched the amount of fish-eats' credit he possessed in pedagogy and in one or more of the standard cultural subjects. Since the paleolithic day was divided into periods between the six meals which the tribe liked to have when food was plentiful, and since fish had formed an important part of the diet from time immemorial, the distance from one fish-eat to another came naturally to be regarded as the proper unit for measuring education.

The elementary teacher's bone had to carry at least fifteen fish-eats' credit in special methods of beginning fish-grabbing, the same amount of credit in the methods of teaching elementary horse-clubbing, but only twelve fish-eats for the corresponding methods course in tiger-scaring. Tiger-scaring was a subject which was not offered until the second year of the elementary school, and it was, therefore, recognized as not demanding quite so much preparatory training as the other two subjects. In addition to special methods, the elementary teacher also needed a certificate on his bone that he had earned thirty fish-eats in the theory and practice of paleolithic education.

The secondary teacher's bone requirements were quite different. He had to have only five fish-eats of special methods in each of the cultural fields in which he taught. If he taught only the various branches of horse-clubbing, he needed only a notation on his bone of special methods in that one field. In general theory and practice of paleolithic education on the secondary level, moreover, he needed only twenty-two and one-half fish-eats. The greater surface of his bone had to be covered by notations concerning strictly subject-matter training in his major and minors. The exact number of fish-eats required varied according to the subject. A major in fish-grabbing required forty-five fish-eats, whereas one in horse-clubbing was only thirty-three. This difference arose from the insistence of the professors of ichthyology that secondary-school graduates entered college ignorant of many of the elements of fish-grabbing. It was therefore necessary, claimed the professors, to devote the first fifteen fish-eats of college work in the subject to teaching what should have been learned in the secondary schools. The professors of equinology, moreover, as soon as they became fully aware of the ichthyologists' success in getting an increase in fish-eats, also protested loudly that they too needed more time for teaching the simplest elements of horse-clubbing to ignorant secondary-school graduates. It was generally conceded by the big chiefs of the tribe, however, that since the ichthyologists had been the first professors to think of making this claim they should be the ones to secure the advantage of extra fish-eats. The equinologists were allotted merely an additional sop of three fish-eats over the standard thirty for college work to quiet their clamor. When the professors of defense engineering, for whose instruction tiger-scaring was a prerequisite, finally awoke to what was going on and made their demand for more fish-eats on the same grounds as their colleagues had cited in the two other fields, the big chiefs rejected the application completely and kept the defense-engineering major at thirty fish-eats.

On the more strictly professional side, professors of paleolithic education gave prospective teachers training in principles and general methods of instruction. These education men faced a very difficult situation from the first. A complete statement of the way in which they fought to overcome their difficulties would be in itself an extensive and important chapter in the history of paleolithic education. It is possible in the time at our disposal merely to outline the main steps in the process whereby the simple subject of pedagogy was transformed into the respectable discipline of education.

In the beginnings of university courses in this field, professors of pedagogy had very little subject matter to teach. They spent most of their time actually trying by precept and example to encourage and direct their students in the work of teaching in elementary and secondary schools. They gave practical hints on the organization and management of classes, described a few rule-of-thumb methods which might be valuable in certain situations, and told stories about the good and bad teachers they had known.

The crude, naïve work of the education professors was regarded with contempt by the subject-matter specialists. It was inevitable that a man who had devoted a lifetime of productive scholarship or systematic speculation to such a problem as The Mystical Element in Sputtering Firebrands as Applied to Tiger-Whiskers or Variations in Thumb-Holds for Grabbing Fish Headed Outward from the Grabber at an Angle of Forty-Five Degrees Plus or Minus Three should be contemptuous of pseudo scholars who were merely trying to show students how to teach.

The academic contempt for pedagogy had a good effect on the education professors. Stung by justified references to their low cultural status, they resolved to make their discipline respectable. With a magnificent display of energy and self-denial, they achieved this goal. First, they organized their subject systematically, breaking it down into respectably small units, erecting barriers to keep professors conventionally isolated from ideas outside their restricted areas, and demanding specialization and more specialization in order to achieve the narrow knowledge and broad ignorance which the paleolithic university demanded of its most truly distinguished faculty members.

Second, they required all members of their group to engage in scientific research in education by counting and measuring quantitatively everything related to education which could be counted and measured. It was here that the professors of education showed the greatest courage and ingenuity. They confronted almost insuperable obstacles in the fact that education dealt with the changing of human minds, a most complex phenomenon. The task of measuring a learning situation involving an unknown number of factors continually modifying each other at unknown rates of speed and with unknown effects was a tremendous one, but the professors did not hesitate to attack it.

Finally, the professors of education worked for academic respectability by making their subject hard to learn. This, too, was a difficult task, but they succeeded admirably by imitating the procedures of their academic colleagues. They organized their subject logically. This necessarily resulted

55

in their giving the abstract and philosophical courses in education first, delaying all practical work in the subject until the student was thoroughly familiar with the accustomed verbalizations of the craft and, thereby, immunized against infection from new ideas. They adopted the lecture method almost exclusively and labored with success to make it an even duller instrument of instruction than it was in the fields of ichthyology, equinology, and defense engineering. They developed a special terminology for their lectures until they were as difficult to understand as any in the strictly cultural fields.

Thus the subject of education became respectable. It had as great a variety of specialists as any field. Some of its professors tried to cover the whole area of the psychology of learning, it is true, but most of them confined their efforts to some more manageable topic like the psychology of learning the preliminary water approach in fish-grabbing. Its research workers were so completely scientific that they could take a large error in the measurement of what they thought maybe was learning in a particular situation and refine it statistically until it seemed to be almost smaller and certainly more respectable than before. Its professors could lecture on modern activity methods of instruction with a scholarly dullness unequalled even by professors of equicephalic anatomy. Their cultured colleagues who had once treated them with contempt were now forced to regard them with suspicious but respectful envy. They had arrived academically.

By the time this goal was reached, however, many of the students whom the professors of education had presumably prepared for teaching were very poor practitioners of the craft. They too tried to be logical, scientific, and respectably dull, and they succeeded in many cases almost as well as their education professors and sometimes even better than their culture professors.

There were a few thoughtful parents of the old New-Fist type who rebelled against this situation.

"But, look here," said the professors of education proudly, "We have succeeded in making our subject academically respectable, haven't we?"

"Why, yes," admitted the radical parents, "but you haven't succeeded in preparing better teachers for the schools. In fact, we are inclined to believe that on some levels of education you have actually made the teaching become steadily worse."

Many of the education professors were intelligent and sensitive men. They squirmed under these charges, and some of them actually began to think about the purposes of education, and a few even went to the length of observing the schools critically. They were struck at once by the artificial character of school learning, by its dissociation from educational objectives, and they set about remedying the situation in various ways.

One group of observers concluded that the chief mistakes in the current educational methods came simply from the circumstance of having too much direction of the learning. "Let the child grow naturally into his learning activities," they advised the teachers. "Let all his purposes and procedures be self-impelled. Without teacher interference or domination, let him always decide what he wants to do, plan what he has purposed, carry out what he has planned, and judge the worth of what he has done."

The teachers were disturbed. "But where, then, do we come in?" they inquired. "If the children are going to do it all, they don't need any teachers."

"Oh, no!" assured the experts. "The teacher is a very necessary guide. He will lead the child in the direction of wise choices of right activities and show him how to engage more intelligently and effectively in those activities in which he would have engaged anyway."

"And suppose," said one teacher guardedly, "that a child wants to engage in cutting up fish-nets. Shall I show him how to do it better than he could without my guidance?"

"You are being facetious," smiled the experts. "Get the real progressive spirit and such questions will not occur to you."

Whereupon the teachers withdrew and consulted among themselves. "It is very clear," suggested one, "that we are still supposed to teach fish-grabbing."

"Yes," agreed another, "but we must not tell the children they *have* to learn fish-grabbing. We must just arrange everything so they themselves will think of learning to grab fish and ask us if they can't do it."

"Ah, I see," said a third, "and then we give them permission and guide—guide—"

The teachers then went back to their classes and proceeded enthusiastically upon this new basis.

"Now, children, what would you like to learn today?" one of them began to a class of twelve-year-olds.

The children stared in astonishment. "We're supposed to learn fish-grabbing, aren't we?" they asked.

"Well—er—not unless you *want* to. What do you really *want* to do?"

"I want to leave school and go to work," announced one of the duller boys.

"Ah, but you *have* to go to school," explained the teacher. "Our compulsory education laws, you know—"

"Who is going to decide whether we pass into the next grade in June?" asked a thin, freckled, myopic girl.

"Why—I am, of course," admitted the teacher.

The members of the class looked at one another a little dubiously, drew a deep collective breath, and then chanted in polite unison, "We want to learn fish-grabbing!"

"Very well, indeed!" said the beaming teacher. "And how are you going to go about learning fish-grabbing?"

"Don't you know?" asked the pupils accusingly.

"Why, yes, of course, but *you* must plan your project yourself."

"All right, then. If you say we got to do it, why, we got to do it. After all, you're the teacher. Let's get into the water here and start."

So the pupils climbed down into the warm water of the heated school tank in which fish-grabbing had been taught for generations and began to go through the motions they had learned in more elementary classes. The teacher stood on the edge of the tank and shouted guidance to the learners. The children laughed and splashed rather happily and caught the new progressive spirit in good style. They caught no fish, of course, but since they had not been catching fish under the traditional instruction, no one thought anything about it for a while.

For some time the experts were satisfied with the results of the new education. The radical parents were quieted, and everything went along smoothly with the school. At last, however, there was another innovation proposed, this time by a teacher.

One of the boys in the school had been playing truant. When he was caught and brought back to school, his teacher asked him what he had been doing during his absence.

"I was playin'," said the boy sullenly.

"Where were you playing?" asked the teacher.

"Down in the crick."

"What were you playing?"

"I—I don't want to tell."

"You *must* tell."

"Well—I—I was playin' fish-grabbin'."

"*Fish-grabbing!*"

"Yes."

"In the *creek?*"

"Uh-huh."

"Well, good gracious! Who ever heard of such a thing! Take off your coat! I could punish mere truancy by having you stay after school, but *this* deserves a whipping. In the *creek!* Indeed! This hurts me worse than it does you, but take that and *that* and THAT! Now you may go to your room."

The teacher might never have made her great theoretical discovery if the punished child had not tried to justify his actions with a final appeal to reason. "Well, my gosh," he sobbed, "the crick is the only place I know where there *is* any fish!"

"That will be enough out of you unless you want another whipping," warned the teacher automatically, but beneath her stern exterior a keen mind was beginning to work at top speed. Forgetful of her surroundings, she paced the floor clenching her fists and breathing audibly through her nose. At length she stopped resolutely and announced her decision. "I will take them down and have them practice fish-grabbing in the creek!"

But when she mentioned this proposal to the school officials, they promptly discharged her. Some of the radical parents were impressed by her vision, however, and suggested that she start a private school for their children—a school of fish-grabbing in a real creek.

The progressive teacher welcomed this opportunity and opened her new school at once. For a while, again, everything went well. The children splashed about in the water happily and the teacher shouted guidance from the bank of the creek.

One day an old independent fisherman who had been absent from the community for many years on an exploring expedition to far-off streams and communities came upon the progressive school in the creek.

"Hello, lady," he said politely to the teacher. "What you got here? A picnic?"

"No, this is a school in session," said the teacher proudly.

"In the *crick*?" asked the old man incredulously.

"Certainly," stated the teacher with some asperity. "It is the Real-Creek School of Fish-Grabbing!"

"That's a good one," laughed the fisherman, "well, so long, I got to be goin'."

"What is so funny about it?" demanded the teacher.

64

"Oh, I was just thinkin'."

"About what?"

"Well, if it's fish you want 'em to grab, it looks to me like what you need is a *real-fish* school instead of just a *real-crick* school."

"Real-fish!"

"Yes, ma'am."

"But how in the world—?"

"Say, lady, would you really like to have them kids grab some real fish?"

"Why—I—but you can't—"

"Can't eh? Well, sister, you just watch your Uncle Dudley."

The fisherman threw his pack on the ground and pulled a small length of seine from it. Calling some of the girls in the school to the bank, he gave them instructions. "I'm goin' to get some fish for you kids to play with," he said. "You got to have some place to keep the fish. There's a hole over there about a jump from the water's edge. You girls get some water jars from your mothers and carry water from the crick to fill that hole."

As the girls scurried off to follow these directions, the fisherman told the boys how to help him operate the seine. With intense interest, the children responded to this task challenge. Within an hour the water-filled hole held about fifty jumping fish.

"I don't see what good that will do," said the teacher critically. "Even in that little hole, those fish are too lively to be caught with the bare hands."

"Just wait," said the fisherman reassuringly, "watch this." He reached into the water with a stout stick and rapped a fish on the head. Again and again he struck until the surface of the pool was covered with dazed fish moving sluggishly or floating helplessly with bellies upward. "There," he said, "now the kids can do some real fish grabbin'."

With ready insight the teacher caught this suggestion. She marshaled the children at once and set them to work on the activity. With whoops of delight the happy youngsters caught the dopey fish and tossed them ashore. The teacher received the fish and threw them back into the pool as quickly and gently as possible, trying economically to make them last as long as they could be used effectively. When a fish became too inactive and flimsy to serve as part of a real life situation, it was laid aside for school lunch purposes and a fresh substitute was secured from the seining grounds. The teacher rapped the new fish over the heads before they were put in the water. She found that it was easier this way to gauge the force of the blow exactly so that the fish would not be completely stunned but only sufficiently anesthetized to make them slow and dopey in their movements.

The professors of education came and watched this experiment with shining eyes. "Please tell us what is happening here," they begged.

"These pupils are learning what they live and living what they learn," said the teacher.

"But they were doing that in the activity school in which you were first teaching. Now you have them actually grabbing fish. It is wonderful— wonderful—but you've got to explain it with names before we can approve it."

"With *names?* You mean—?"

"We mean *technically*. Now technically, what do you say this is?"

The teacher thought hard. "It is *creative*," she announced finally, "creative fish-grabbing. That's what it is. The children want to grab fish, they plan to grab them, they actually grab them—and right there is the creative part—you see?"

The professors all nodded hard and the most distinguished one even added a "Yes, yes."

"Yes, the children get in there and *create* opportunities to catch fish by grabbing," continued the teacher enthusiastically. "They create the school pool, the school water, and really they create the school fish—well the essence of the whole thing is *creativeness*—you see—and that is why we are going to call this experimental institution the *School of Creative Fish-Grabbing*. The creative part is the heart of the whole movement—just to catch fish—bah!—that's nothing—but to grab fish *creatively*—ah! That is something!"

All the professors nodded again, and the most distinguished one added an "Ah yes."

The concept of real fish-grabbing spread like wildfire. Even the teachers in the school from which the founder of creative fish-grabbing had been fired were forced to give in to a demand for real fish in the classroom. The parents came to them and said, "Our children don't learn to grab fish with the bare hands any more under this present system than they did in the old days. They are impertinent to us at home, moreover, claiming that they must always do as they please in order to develop integrated personalities."

"They *must* have integrated personalities," said the teachers sternly.

"Yes, we know," admitted the parents, "but, for goodness' sakes, get 'em to integrate their personalities around some real fish-grabbing instead of just around raising hell at home."

So the teachers of the school bought some fish, tapped them over the head, put them in the school tank, and started classes in real fish-grabbing.

The director of the creative school sniffed at the whole proceeding. "Huh," she scoffed, "call that tank a *natural* situation! Nonsense! It is artificial! It's too far from the creek. You can't get a *creative* situation except in a natural setting."

The teachers who were thus criticized knew that there was no adequate answer to this indictment. They knew that the situation in their school *was* artificial. The fish in the tank were a long way from the creek. That was the rub. And yet if they tried a hole down by the creek they would be copying the director of the School of Creative Fish-Grabbing, a person who had been discharged from their school.

One day as the principal of the tank school sat gloomily watching the children toss fish around, he was approached by a man who introduced himself as an alumnus of the institution.

"I haven't been back here for twenty years," said the old grad amiably.

"No?" responded the principal, wondering how soon he could get rid of the fellow.

"Yes," continued the alumnus. "I've been traveling—away down south—I'm a hunter, you know—"

The principal ceased to listen but just set himself to nodding politely while thinking over the shame of running an uncreative school.

After an interval, however, something in the steady flow of the visitor's conversation began to hammer for attention in the principal's consciousness. "Yes, sir," the traveler was saying, "down there in that desert, there are at least two tigers left, maybe more—real saber-tooth tigers—and a man could—"

"What!" cried the principal, as the full educational significance of the statement flashed over him. "What! Actual *living* tigers!"

"Yes, sir. Real honest-to-God tigers."

"Oh, well,"—the principal sank back into his accustomed dejection once more—"it couldn't be done anyway."

"What couldn't be done?" asked the traveler.

"Use these tigers as educational materials. I thought for a minute we might, but now I see it can't be done. We couldn't catch those tigers in the first place, and if we caught them we couldn't make them dopey by just rapping them over the head—probably just make them angry—no, I see it's impossible."

"Well, I don't know about that," said the alumnus aggressively. "I could catch 'em—put 'em in a cage—bring 'em up here. It would cost money, of course, but—"

"Cage!" The principal snapped his fingers, all his gloom vanishing again in a moment. "Cage!

Now I see how it can be done. Money? We'll get you the money!"

This was the beginning of the second great institution of progressive paleolithic education. The Real-Tiger School, it was called. Admiring teachers and professors of education came for many days' journeys to see the children of this school line up every morning and wave torches in the faces of two real saber-tooth tigers. The two old tigers, last of their race, toothless, deaf, almost blind, were tired. They asked only to be left in peace in their declining years. They blinked wearily at the children who squealed and waved firebrands before the cage. They did not like this activity. It was too tiresome for aged tigers.

But the tigers were alone in this attitude. Everybody else liked it. The children had fun. The teachers found the activity stimulating. Even the radical parents had to admit that here was an achievement whose progressiveness could not be denied. The tigers were real and very rare. Their rarity seemed somehow to make their reality all the more meaningful.

The general verdict was expressed cleverly and profoundly by the most distinguished education professor. "This Real-Tiger School," he announced, after a thorough investigation, "is the real thing. To the casual observer, these children may appear just to be waving firebrands at a couple of caged tigers, but to me they are *learning what they live and living what they learn!*"

IV · HIGHER PALEOLITHIC EDUCATION

"I SEE that the president of the University of Oskaloosa has broken into print again," I remarked.

"What does he appear to have on his young mind now?" asked Dr. Peddiwell.

"He is concerned about the plight of higher education in America," I said.

"And well he might be," remarked the professor approvingly. "Does he say what he is going to do about it?"

"Yes. He is going to make it rational, systematic, orderly."

"Oh, ho! And a very proper thing to try to do, and if he actually did do that, it would certainly be a wholesome lesson to it. How is he going to establish order in higher education?"

"He is going to make the study of metaphysics pervade the whole university. Not information but pure thought is going to be the university's aim."

"A wonderful contribution! Yes, sir—a plan worthy of the best paleolithic thinking and in fact highly reminiscent of the university reform which ushered in the golden age of paleolithic culture."

"Yes, sir?" I breathed softly and waited for the lecture which I could see was on its way.

The paleolithic university, like those of other countries and times (began Dr. Peddiwell), was started for magical reasons. Ordinarily schools gave enough education as long as subjects were taught for their practical values only, but as soon as esoteric knowledge was developed for its own hocus-pocus sake, universities became necessary.

The paleolithic university was really founded the day the paleolithic creek got too muddy for fish to be caught in it with the bare hands. From that time forward, fish-grabbing had to be taught for general cultural or magical reasons, and it was inevitable that the university should be developed for that purpose.

The paleolithic professions of sorcery, chieftainship, and hunting engineering were learned professions requiring university training from the first simply because they were magical professions from the first. The medicine men cast out evil spirits and treated disease, to some extent, by science and common sense but mostly by magic and charm. The chiefs ruled the people, a little by understanding them but a lot by hexing them. Antelope, bears, and fish were caught with snares, traps, and nets in a certain limited sense, but in the more important sense of the supernaturally real, they were caught by prayers and incantations.

Thus professional education and the higher magical education went together in paleolithic times for very good and logical reasons, just as they have gone together ever since. Our young friend, the president of the University of Oskaloosa, is worried by this circumstance. The dear boy lacks historical background, or he would see that any profession which has been saturated with magic throughout its history cannot be divorced from the

"Dreading to have illiterate medicine men when our present torch-butt kissers shall lie in the Dust."

one educational institution which is devoted to the theory and practice of magic.

The patheolithic university started with a simple enough goal. Because tiger-scaring had once been the most dangerous and dramatic activity in tribal experience, the fundamental passes in the medicine man's ritual were derived from the elementary work in that subject. As tigers became extinct, and the subject of tiger-scaring became purely esoteric, medicine men took over the field entirely. They became the select body of adepts and specialists that the discipline had to have in order to be truly esoteric.

The motto of the university stated the goal quite clearly: "*That we may have smooth tiger-scaring when our present medicine men shall lie in the dust.*"

In addition to having a strictly magical purpose, the paleolithic university also had magical subjects. From the very beginning of the university, the value of the education it gave was determined by reference to the magical properties of various subjects rather than by any attempts to discover real changes in students. Thus one subject was considered to give a double dose of magic, while another might give only one-tenth of a dose. Indeed, there were certain subjects which were thought to be anti-magical in their effects.

The whole theory of positive and negative culture arose from these attempts to rate magic dosages in the university. It was not enough for the university to provide positive culture in the way of subjects with approved magic ratings; it must also see to it that no subjects with negative culture values were left lying around where students might be exposed to them.

This system of magic-value ratings for various subjects would have worked much better if the university authorities could only have standardized the dosages. They were unable to do this, however, and the result was an unending struggle between the subject-magic haves and the have-nots.

As we have already seen, tiger-scaring was the first sacred subject. It ruled the university roost for a long time. No one could undertake preparation for any profession without first becoming saturated with the spirit of this discipline, learning all its chants and exorcisms, and mastering all its holy passes and spells.

Perhaps this happy arrangement would have lasted forever, had not the professors of tiger-scaring attempted to advance their subject. If they could only have been satisfied to teach students to go through the sacred motions, all would have been well. As it was, however, although most of the professors were willing to get along with the barest minimum of mental and physical work, there were a few energetic and conscientious professors who created all the difficulty. These hard-working ones knew that professors were supposed to advance their subjects. They knew, furthermore, that a subject like tiger-scaring, which was already considered to be perfect, could not very well be advanced by research. Research looked for new answers; a magical subject already had answers which it was heresy to doubt.

The tiger-scaring professors were forced to do what the professors of any truly holy subject have to do—they had to make greater and greater claims for the magic power of their subject while fighting off the pretensions of lesser subjects to have some magic influence.

So it happened that tiger-scaring, which had once been a useful and relatively simple safety measure and later a kind of moderately magical device for developing general courage in children, became a sovereign remedy for all intellectual and spiritual ills. As nothing else could do, it made men wise and noble and just. It was a touchstone of membership in the tribal elite. It was a guarantee of civic rectitude and private morality alike. It was the subject without which no man could hope to look a difficult fact in the face.

When other professors began to suggest magic claims for their subjects, the tiger-scaring specialists rose to new heights of aggressive reverence for their field. They leaped from claim to claim, rising even higher, until at last they came out flat-footed with the assertion that every detail of the tiger-scaring ritual had been set in the beginning of time by the Great Mystery himself.

At first this claim was pretty generally accepted. Nobody dared to shake his head, be it ever so slightly, at a subject whose claims everybody was required to know and revere. At last, however, the inevitable happened. A professor of ichthyology attacked this newest claim with vigor and courage. He had evidence to support his attack, moreover, and this made the resulting discussion doubly painful in view of the fact that a truly magic subject never requires evidence to support its claims.

The revolting professor had received his appointment by mistake. He had never had the required basic training in tiger-scaring to be a professor of any kind, but through carelessness on the part of the authorities he was allowed to take the most advanced work in general fish-grabbing and the special graduate training in ichthyology. Then, to cap the matter in final absurdity, the man was appointed professor. Of course, a circumstance of this sort could not be kept secret for long. The new professor's colleagues found that he had never secured a single fish-eat in tiger-scaring beyond the secondary level. From that time forward, they paid no attention to his researches, reduced his teaching opportunities to a minimum, and tried their best to keep him from doing too much harm to the good name of the university.

This was the mean and jealous person who started the revolt against the supremacy of tiger-scarers in the university curriculum. He studied the various details of the tiger-scaring routine and finally came forward with sworn statements from a hundred aged tribesmen that the practice of kissing the butt of the torch before beginning the standard tiger-scaring rites had been unknown fifty years before. He produced various other witnesses, moreover, who testified that the practice of torch-butt kissing had been introduced originally by a tiger-scaring assistant at the university who had thought thereby to make symbolic confession of profane love for his landlady's daughter.

The whole paleolithic world was rocked by these charges. The erring professor and the few of his students and colleagues who were tainted at all by his heresy were summarily discharged from the university and forever barred from holding further offices of trust and responsibility. No professors, medicine men, chiefs, or engineers were allowed to take new offices or retain the posts they already had until they subscribed to the following oath; "I do solemnly abjure, detest, and condemn as a deadly error the doctrine that kissing the torch butt was not started by osculation of the Great Mystery himself, and I do solemnly swear that I will oppose this heresy with all my strength and that I will at all times do my utmost to extirpate the root and branch of this and all other errors which are judged by my superiors to be contrary to the theory and practice of tiger-scaring as determined by the paleolithic laws and the regulations of our paleolithic university."

With all these safeguards around the subject of tiger-scaring, it seems incredible that any other subject should ever have been able to attain magic status, but horse-clubbing was fortunate enough to do it in a relatively short time, and fish-grabbing followed soon thereafter. The professors of both these fields followed the standard practice of making stronger and stronger magic claims for their respective subjects until they had developed almost as much reverence for them as had ever been commanded for tiger-scaring in its heyday. The new magic claimants fought each other as much as the older field had ever fought them, moreover, so that each of the three main subjects spent much of its energy in trying to retain as much magic prestige as possible and at the same time keep its two rivals in subordinate positions.

The battle to keep the university curriculum confined to one, two, or a few magical subjects was lost almost before it was well started, however. The followers of one subject could make just as many magic claims for it as could those of another, and it was not long before a large number of subjects were claimed by their supporters to be magically cultural. The only subjects which lacked cultural respectability were those which were studied for their practical effect on the behavier of learners. These subjects remained in a suspected and inferior category, therefore, because they did not pretend to have magic power. Thus the only real disgrace in the university curriculum was seen to be the disgrace of being practical. To modify human behavior for some real purpose kept a subject from becoming truly sacred.

There were three great reform movements in the history of the paleolithic university. The first reform started with the development of the free-magic system of choosing subjects for the students in place of the original one-magic system which required all learners to go through the same routine. The free-magic arrangement was based on the premise that all approved university subjects were of similar magic virtue. It followed unerringly, therefore, that each student might as well select his own particular dosage. Only the size of the dose was prescribed. Its character was left to free choice. The free-magic system was much appreciated by administrators and professors alike. It helped the administrators by protecting them from the necessity of making decisions about the values of subjects, and it helped the professors by protecting their feelings through assuming that all subjects were equally magical.

Actually the system of free-magic could not be worked by university professors, and since the details of all university administration were handled by professors, aided by clerks and stenographers who were more professorially minded than the professors themselves, the system broke down of its own administrative weight. By a series of interdepartmental deals, these professors kept modifying the free-magic system until they had an arrangement whereby the only choice a student had was the choice of department. After making that choice he was bound rigidly to follow the departmental magic without deviation. If he selected horse-clubbing, for example, all the power of all the professors, clerks, and stenographers in the department of horse-clubbing was thrown in the direction of making him learn as many details of the horse-clubbing magic as could possibly be forced on him. The professors of other departments, in paleolithic senate meetings, might force some symbolic gesture toward the old free-magic system by requiring fifteen fish-eats for a minor and perhaps as much as twenty fish-eats for free choice, but the sheer weight of ninety-five fish-eats would remain to be devoted exclusively to horse-clubbing and related subjects. If any department did not have ninety-five fish-eats of instruction to offer in its field, the shame of being thus delinquent would soon bring its course offerings up to standard.

The chief effect of the major-magic system was to make all departments suspicious of one another. The quality of instruction remained just as good as it had been under the free-magic regime or even under the original one-magic system, however. When the goal of instruction was a magical effect, one kind of spell or incantation worked just about as well as another so long as it was applied with the proper faith and fervor.

The third main university reform came with the ushering in of the general-magic system. This was really an attempt to get back to the original one-magic basis without disturbing the devotees of various subjects. It was the result of the old deep-seated yearning for some really powerful educational medicine, something that would be equally good for any one of a variety of ills. One leader suggested tiger-scaring, of course, as the proper basis for showing all students how to think, not what to think.

"Tiger-scaring is the basic discipline," he said. "Every motion of horse-clubbing, every step in fish-grabbing—they all go back to that first activity in tiger-scaring, kissing the torch butt. Do you know any one who is thoroughly grounded in any science or social science who has not been subjected to the mental and emotional discipline involved in kissing that butt? No, you do not. If, in any particular case, you think you do, I can show you quickly enough where the lack of basic education will show up in that case. If it appears nowhere else, it will be bound to show up in an ignorance of the technique of torch-butt kissing.''

Other leaders made similar claims for horse-clubbing and fish-grabbing until the great university chiefs decided that all three of these subjects should be called "general-magic" and be given a place of honor in the new university education.

At this point an obscure professor, walking along the creek for recreation one afternoon, fell and hit his head on a rock. His bumps of caution and memory were badly damaged. When he was released from the hospital to return to his university duties, although he appeared superficially to be normal again, he soon gave evidence of the real severity of his head injuries. Freed from the restraint of his usual sense of caution and unhampered by memory of what a university was like, he began to go around the campus asking questions so naïve as to be practically psychopathic.

"Is a university a kind of school?" he would often begin.

"Yes," his colleagues would tell him pityingly, "A university is a school, an advanced school, a school where the teachers know much more than do the teachers in ordinary schools, but still a kind of a school."

"Schools are educational institutions, aren't they?"

"Of course."

"And is education supposed to change people?"

"Certainly."

"Is it supposed to make them better or worse?"

"Better, naturally."

"Then in order to know what to do with our students in the university, we must discover how to treat them so that they will become better?"

"Well, yes, better, more efficient, more competent intellectually. We must teach them *how* to think, *not what* to think."

"A student can become better, more efficient, more intelligent only with respect to the social environment in which he operates?"

"Why—er—yes, I suppose so."

"Then in order to determine what our university curriculum should be, we must first decide what our society should be?"

"Oh, no! Certainly not! That would be the blueprint of a future social order. That would be teaching them *what* to think. Besides, you would be pretending to know what is going to happen tomorrow. Only the Great Mystery knows what is going to happen tomorrow. Are you setting yourself up to be the Great Mystery? You will be lucky not to be struck dead for that impiety!"

"I don't see anything so wrong about attempting to predict what is going to happen tomorrow. If I teach my students tiger-scaring just as university professors have been doing for the Great Mystery knows how many years, will I not, in effect, be predicting that those students are going to be in a society tomorrow in which tiger-scaring will be a very valuable thing for them to know?"

"Ah, now you are talking sense," shouted all the professors. "Tiger-scaring *is* good general magic; it is positive culture plus. You stick to tiger-scaring and you'll wear academic diamonds yet."

The questioning professor's head still hurt, but that was partly a result of having hit it pretty hard on a rock.

V · EDUCATION AND PALEOLITHIC SECURITY

 "THE American Federation of Teachers is an unprofessional organization," I asserted flatly, taking a firm grip on the bar rail.

"Indeed," commented Dr. Pediwell politely, "and why do you make this statement so vehemently, my young friend?"

"Because I realize the danger to our profession in some of the things which the teachers' union is trying to do."

"One thing, for instance?"

"Well, to ally themselves with labor, for example. That is a shameful thing."

"Ah, *shameful.* A rather severe word, don't you think?"

"It is a correct word. They become partisan when they align themselves with any particular group—organized labor! It is terrible. It is unprofessional."

"Ah, yes. Quite, quite. Would you say *un-American* too?"

"Un-American? Well—uh—I don't know—"

"These teachers, you know, they align themselves with all sorts of impossible groups. Some of them are Methodists, some are members of chambers of commerce, and some are even reserve officers. It is all quite unprofessional, I agree, un-American too."

"I—I don't see, Doctor, exactly what—"

"No, you don't see, and the reason you don't see is because you lack historical perspective and background. You look at our present difficulties and fail to see the relationship between them and the task of education. You don't remember how clearly that relationship was developed and ignored in paleolithic times. Why don't you use the lessons of history?"

"Because I don't know the lessons of history," I admitted humbly.

"Very well, then," said the professor, "let us find chairs somewhere along this row of lying mirrors, and I shall teach you one of those lessons to the best of my ability."

The paleolithic tribesmen (said Dr. Peddiwell) were cursed with technical intelligence. If they had been somewhat more stupid, they would never have had economic difficulties. As it was, however, their clever inventions of fishnets, antelope snares, and bear pits gave them no end of trouble.

Their chief difficulties came from the ease with which they could make a living under the new system. In the old days practically all the tribe, old and young, had to work hard at grabbing fish, clubbing horses, and scaring tigers. Now, three or four men could catch enough fish in one day to feed the tribe for a week. One man could attend to a whole string of antelope snares which, with relatively little effort, would produce more meat and skins than twenty horse-clubbers could have secured in the same length of time in the old days by the severest labor. A properly constructed bear pit lasted indefinitely, moreover, and after each trail was guarded with one, there was nothing to do but kill the trapped bears and add their great bulk of meat and skins to an already overflowing store.

In time, however, the wise old men of the tribe solved this difficulty. They did it by developing certain rules which they derived from studying the actions of the more clever members of the tribe.

For example, after fishnets had been generally developed and everybody came to use them, it was often very difficult to find a vacant place in the stream to fish. Thus fishing no longer offered merely a technological problem but also a problem in the adjustment of social relations. Indeed it seemed that the more skillful a man learned to be in fishing the harder it was for him to operate without finding his fellows in his way and walking on their toes.

One of the shrewdest fishermen of the tribe, finding himself so crowded by other fishermen that he could not set and draw his net to best advantage, solved the problem by devising a system of ownership of fishing rights. One morning, as the result of unusually good luck the day before, he round that he had five fish more than his family had been able to eat. At first he thought that he would merely take a day off and not fish at all, since five fish would feed his family adequately for the day, but he liked to fish, and the thought of missing the activity for one day saddened him. "How can I get rid of these fish and at the same time get a chance to catch some more?" he asked himself.

As he was thinking over this problem, he watched the fisherman on his right. This man was not a very skillful operator. He set his net clumsily and brought it in too slowly. "I could catch more fish than that man in any hole in the creek," said the clever fisherman to himself. "If I had his hole and mine too, I could catch twice as many fish as I catch now, and probably four times as many as that slow fisherman catches."

So the clever fisherman made the slow fisherman a proposition. "I'll give you these five fish," he offered, "if you will lay off fishing today and let me fish in your section of the creek."

"Well," said the slow fisherman doubtfully, "I don't know for sure whether that's a good bargain.

Maybe I could catch ten or twenty fish if I stayed here and worked."

"Yes, maybe you could," said the smart fisherman, "and then, again, maybe you couldn't. Maybe you'd catch only five fish or four, or maybe you'd catch none at all. How many did you catch yesterday?"

"Three."

"Ah, ha! And the day before?"

"Well, it was a bad day, too rainy—I didn't get *any*."

"Ah, *ha!* There you are."

"But the day before *that* I got twelve!"

"Uh-huh, in other words you averaged just five fish a day, just what I propose to give you. You must remember, too, that you worked hard for those fish, and I am going to give you five fish without your doing a lick of work."

The slow fisherman could not count beyond twenty, the number of fingers and toes he had to work with arithmetically, and the process of dividing fifteen by five was altogether too advanced for him, but he was impressed by the mathematical competence of the clever fisherman and by the undeniable fact that he would be *sure* of five fish without any expenditure of care or energy. Because he wanted security more than he wanted to be enterprising and because also he was not very intelligent, he accepted the five fish, told all the tribesmen that his place in the creek was to be held for the day by the smart fisherman, and retired to his cave to sleep away his new-found leisure.

The smart fisherman had very good luck in his double allotment of space. He caught twenty fish more than his family needed to eat. The next day, therefore, he was ready with a new proposition to his slower comrade. "Let me give you a lot of fish," he said, "for the use of your fishing ground always."

"*Always*," repeated the slow fisherman, startled by the proposal. "But what would I *do*? I have to fish somewhere, don't I?"

"No, you don't," the smart fisherman assured him. "All you have to do is to sit and take in the fish I bring to you."

"How many fish will you bring me?"

"I will bring you five fish a day."

"Will you do that forever?"

"Well, practically forever. I'll bring you five fish every day until I have brought you ten times ten times ten fish. You can see yourself that it will take a very long time to pay up a debt like that at the rate of five fish a day. In the meantime you can snare antelopes or trap bears the same as anybody else. You'll be rich, for you can have as much meat and skins as anybody for your work and in addition you will have five fish a day rolling in without your ever having even so much as to lift your hand."

To one of the slow fisherman's limited mathematical competence, *ten times ten times ten* sounded like a quantity of the order that the French war debt would sound to the average citizen today. All the slow fisherman could see ahead of him when he listened to those figures was a rosy security stretching far into the future. He accepted the proposal with alacrity, therefore, and the chief of the tribe was called in to scratch a statement of the bargain on the sacred bone which was used for that purpose.

The clever fisherman was so successful with his catches that within a few days he felt able to make similar arrangements with another slow fisherman. Finding that he prospered on this venture too, he soon had the rights to half a dozen fishing holes. The fish tended to crowd away from the more heavily fished part of the stream into the relatively quiet territory of the smart fisherman's six-man stretch of water. He was consequently able to catch ten times as many fish in six holes as he had before caught in one.

In less than seven months the smart fisherman had paid completely for the first individual fishing right he had bought, and before the end of the year he had finished paying for six and had contracted to buy ten more. Two of the remaining fishermen who were clever enough to see the advantages of private ownership and energetic enough to seize those advantages began to follow the same procedure. At the end of very few years the fishing industry was owned and operated by three great fish chiefs.

The fishermen who sold their stream rights were able to work for a while in the antelope and bear industries, but they crowded the trails so much that the process of developing private ownership of hunting rights was thereby hastened. Again the slower, more stupid, more luckless, mathematically more inept tribesmen accepted a temporary combination of security and leisure and turned over their trail rights to a few aggressive, energetic, lucky, and clever men who built up the antelope and bear industries as the fish chiefs had built up the fishing industry.

Of course the three great fish chiefs soon came to the place in the expansion of their activities where they were unable, even with the help of all members of their families, to keep all their nets in operation. They began to hire propertyless men to operate their nets and smoke their fish. They paid an adult worker two fish a day. When it was pointed out to them that the average family had to have five fish a day barely to exist, the chiefs replied that the average family had two adults and three children, that the two adults could earn four fish a day, and that the children however small and weak ought to be able to do half the work of an adult and thus earn the remaining fish needed for the family sustenance.

This arrangement was actually possible for a few families in the earlier stages of the development of the industry. For a while the great fish chiefs hired all the help they could get, men, women, children. They kept the nets working even at night on some occasions. The great chiefs sat on the bank of the stream, paid out wages, and watched the steadily growing pile of smoked fish.

After this boom had gone on a little time, however, the fish chiefs had great difficulty in getting rid of their wealth of fish. Sometimes they traded a few fish for antelope and bear hides, sometimes they gave a lot of fish for bear-tooth necklaces wherewith to adorn their wives and daughters, but still their fish piles grew and grew. They had to catch fewer fish. They reduced the amount of their fishing, throwing their workers out of jobs. The men who remained on their pay rolls were attempting to feed five-fish-per-day families on two fish. The unemployed ate no fish at all but tried to subsist on berries or an occasional bite of antelope or bear meat.

The wise old men who were the main chiefs of the tribe saw that something would have to be done, so they made a rule that any fish chief who would give the whole tribe a pile of fish as high as a man might buy the exclusive right to make fishnets in his neighborhood. All three fish chiefs immediately accepted this offer and turned over their piles of fish to the tribal government. The government began to give one-half fish a day to every man who was unemployed and one-quarter of a fish for every woman and child he had in his family. Thus a family of two adults and three children which needed five fish to live on in the old days and which recently had tried to get along on two fish, now tried to get along on one and one-half fish. The fish chiefs, on the other hand, were now entirely safe in the control of the industry. The tools of production as well as the places in which to fish were entirely in their hands.

The antelope and bear chiefs were impressed with the success of the fish chiefs, so they went to the great rulers of the tribe and asked very respectfully, "Do not the laws which you wise old men make apply everywhere to everybody with equal force?"

The old men took counsel with one another and then answered solemnly, "It is true that the laws which we make are universal. It is an essential mark of wisdom to know much more than any single case can show. We are wise. We made these laws. Therefore they are universal. They apply to any case. Incidentally, if it is of interest to you, they are eternal too."

"Good," said the smooth antelope-snarers and bear-pit-watchers. "We know now how to become great chiefs and really develop our industries. We shall compete with one another in free and open business."

"May the best men win," said the rulers.

Thus the antelope and bear industries were developed along the lines which had been laid down in the fishing industry. The piles of fish, meat, and skins grew higher and higher, and the long lines of unemployed waiting for their tribal ration became bigger and bigger.

The stores of fish, meat, and skins became so large, however, that the great industrial chiefs

THE SABER-TOOTH CURRICULUM

could not find any use for them. They loaned fish and meat, they rented skins, always for the price of more fish, meat, and skins, and so finally they had to close down their industries altogether and wait for the accumulated piles of wealth to rot.

Now everyone was out of work, and everyone except the few great fish, antelope, and bear chiefs were out of food too. The tribal authorities used up their small store of relief provisions very quickly. The unemployed tribesmen wandered idly up and down the creek staring hungrily at the rich stores of food and covering. Wild-eyed radicals climbed upon rocks and began to make inflammatory speeches. The poor people listened to these stupid and insane statements until they were actually ready to rush the piles of food and skins and take by force what they needed for themselves and their families to eat and wear. The situation was desperate, as all the clever tribal rulers and industrial chiefs could readily see.

The rulers were equal to this emergency, however. They called all the chiefs into consultation and taxed them as follows. Every fish chief had to pay the tribal authorities one fish out of every hundred he caught. All persons who ate fish, moreover, had to give the tribal authorities two hundredths of a fish for every fish they ate. Similar taxes were levied on antelope and bear meat and skins. With the food and covering thus secured, the tribal government was enabled to resume relief to the unemployed. A great economic crisis was thus averted.

One day a demented tribesman got upon a rock by the creek bed and addressed his fellows in the following words. "The whole trouble with our economic system lies in those original rules which were figured out by some smart boys at the expense of some dumb boys and then adopted by the chiefs just because the smart boys belonged to their gang. Let's change those rules," he suggested.

"How would you change them?" asked some of his hearers.

"Let's just use our common sense and put everybody back to work on fishing, antelope-snaring, and bear-pit digging and watching," said the orator. "Maybe there are some other things that could be found for us to do. Anyway, let's all get

to work and let's all eat and wear whatever we can
get."

His hearers looked at each other wonderingly.
They knew there was something very bad in this
man's suggestions, but at first they couldn't figure
out what it really was.

The Daughters of Barehanded Fish-Grabbers,
the members of the Loyal Order of Stuffed-Horse
Clubs, and the Sons of Saber-Tooth Veterans
heard of the man's statements, however. They
came and listened to him. They saw what was
wrong with him and his proposal, and they knew
immediately how to handle him.

"You are preaching an un-paleolithic ism," they
said to the demented worker. When he persisted,
they warned him, "Shut up or we will duck you
in the creek."

Most of the man's hearers now saw plainly
what was wrong with him and his argument. "We
see through you now," they shouted. "Shut up or
we will duck you in the creek."

"I stand on my rights as a paleolithic tribesman," began the worker, "and I am merely telling
you what I think would be a good and wise and

expedient thing to do. Is it a crime for me to tell you that?"

Then he started to repeat his suggestions for improving the life of the tribe, but when he came to the place where he actually came right out and proposed that the rules of the wise old men should be changed, the good citizens standing there grabbed him and ducked him and held him under water until he promised faithfully to behave himself in the future.

A teacher who had been standing in the crowd and observing this exciting event asked his fellow teachers about it next morning. "In education shouldn't we do something definite, have something clearly in mind, have a particular goal which will modify the behavior of our people so that they can arrange some system of hunting and fishing that will keep them better from starvation?"

"We can teach them *how* to think, *not what* to think," chanted his fellow teachers in unison.

"But we have plenty of fish, meat, and skins for everybody to have enough to eat and wear if they only knew enough to eat and wear them," insisted the inquiring teacher. "Surely we teachers can help the people to educate themselves sufficiently to attain such a simple goal as that."

Whereupon his fellow teachers hung their heads and kicked their toes in the sand embarrassedly. Finally the oldest and wisest teacher of the lot spoke the sentiment of the whole group.

"You'd better not repeat that in any of your classes," he said warningly. "You'll get your neck out too *far*—you'll get your ears slapped *down*—you'll get *fired*, that's what *you'll* get. School teachers are not supposed to change people's ways so much that the people will change the rules of the wise old men, and don't you forget that. Don't you forget *that*, just as long as the wise old men run the schools, or the first thing you know you'll be on the outside looking in."

The inquiring teacher thereupon hung *his* head, dug *his* toes in the sand, and resolved to mend his ways. He kept his resolution faithfully, and as a result he was not fired until the economic difficulty in which the tribe found itself became so grave that all schools had to run on half the number of fish they had been granted in the past.

VI · THE PALEOLITHIC YOUTH PROBLEM

 "THE youth commission has got out a new report," I announced, handing a copy of the article to Dr. Peddiwell.

"Ah, yes," he murmured, without looking at the report, "it is indeed a sad situation, a sad situation."

"What do you mean, a *sad situation?*" I demanded.

"Ah, yes," he continued placidly, "a sad situation and one not susceptible to treatment by modern educators."

"What do you mean, *not susceptible to treatment by educators?*"

"When the average educator finally, after due deliberation, heart searchings, and conferences with the president of the First National Bank and the secretary of the Chamber of Commerce, decides that it would be all right, proper, educationally correct, to try to get over a wall which seems to be in the road of progress, he always attempts to make a nice little ladder by which he may crawl over the wall cautiously."

"Well, what's wrong with that?"

"Nothing is wrong with it, except that we need a lot of educators who can at least recognize that there are other ways of getting over that wall."

"What way, for instance?"

"We need educators who will see the possibility occasionally of getting some nice big sticks of dynamite, planting them in neat holes at the base of the wall, producing a spark at the right moment, and blowing the whole works to—er—small pieces."

"But I don't see—"

"Of course you don't see, and the reason why you don't is because you lack historical background, the background that gives perspective. You look at our present youth problem and the various ingenious proposals for its solution, and you forget that the problem was equally distressing in paleolithic days and was solved in equally ingenious fashions."

"Yes, I do forget. Go ahead, Professor."

With this introduction and stimulus, Dr. Peddiwell settled himself in his chair, took a firm grip on his glass, and launched into the following lecture.

During the depression caused by having too much fish, meat, and skins, the paleolithic youth problem was very acute. It was hard enough for the older members of the tribe to secure work in the fish, antelope and bear industries, but the young adults had no chance for work at all. After studying the fundamentals of fish-grabbing, horse-clubbing, and tiger-scaring in the elementary schools, the young people went into the secondary schools and took advanced work in the same subjects, until at about the age of eighteen it was thought best for them to finish their secondary education. They all wanted to go to the paleolithic university and learn to become medicine men, chiefs, and engineers, but most of them could never hope to secure the necessary fish, meat, and skins to pay for this higher education. Many of those who did go to the university found it difficult to get places in their professions after they were graduated.

A few young people tried to make a living by sneaking out at night and stealing fish from the nets or meat from the snares of the great chiefs, but this was a very dangerous practice. The great majority were too honest to do anything of this sort. They wandered idly about, getting the necessary minimum of food and skins from their parents or from the relief grants allotted to them by the wise rulers of the tribe.

A temporary occupation for the young adults was found in a pile of smooth pebbles and rocks ranging in size from marbles to bowling balls. This rock pile was up on the hill back of the tribal caves. Some of the more energetic young people began to go up to the rock pile every day and play various games with the stones there. Other young men and women who had completed their formal education and who were unemployed soon followed. It was not long before most of the

"Is it possible that they are just monkeying with those rocks?"

115

young adults of the tribe knew how to amuse
themselves on the youth rock pile, and some of
them were quite adept at it.

Various games were played at the rock pile.
Some young people played marbles with pebbles,
others used somewhat larger stones for a kind of
billiard game on the ground, and still others used
the largest stones for bowling balls. Certain of the
less athletic young persons with an eye for form
and color arranged various piles of rocks according
to their shapes and tints or made patterns and
designs in rock walls and borders.

More and more youths came up the hill to play
with rocks as more and more games were invented to utilize them. Even some of the older
unemployed people, finding time heavy on their
hands, followed the young people up the hill and
adopted this method of using their leisure. At
times the rock pile was so crowded that players
had to take turns in order to get the use of even a
small rock.

Occasionally a few of the more dangerously
discontented young people would flare up in resentment at what appeared to them to be the

purposelessness and uselessness of their activities. Some of them even had the temerity to say, "We have a right to work for ourselves and our tribe. Are we to be kept forever in this baby play with rocks? This was the sort of thing the children of the tribe were doing ages ago when the great and wise New-Fist saw them and invented the first educational system to give them something useful to do, to prepare them for *work*. What this tribe needs is not more leisure but more work. Some of it can be truly recreational work, but none of it should be this degrading busy-ness with play designed merely to keep us from thinking too much about our difficulties. Let us take a bunch of these stones down the hill and use them to break the antiquated rules of the medicine men! Maybe, before we get through, we can use some of these rocks to break a few heads! Maybe that's the way to get some action on the changed ways this tribe needs!"

Most of the persons on the youth rock pile were good paleolithics of the best boy- and girl-trapper type, however. They reported these cases of unrest to the medicine men and assured the authorities that they knew they could get nowhere by being radical in the slightest degree.

The wise rulers of the tribe saw the possibility of danger, nevertheless, and resolved to take steps well in advance to solve the youth problem before it became too embarrassing. After considering various ways in which they might acquire the necessary information and skill to deal with the problem, they decided to use the method of a general conference. They had great faith in the conference method of attaining wisdom and developing techniques. So they began by appointing a paleolithic youth commission and calling it into immediate session.

The members of the youth commission represented all the most important elements in the tribe. The fish, antelope, and bear chiefs sent hired men to act as their mouthpieces. Some of the greatest professors of fish-grabbing, horse-clubbing, and tiger-scaring were there. The federated brotherhoods of fishnet, antelope-snare, and bear-pit workers were represented by their great president who had done so much to keep them contented with the rules of the medicine men. The young people themselves, of course, were not represented by any of their number, as it was well understood that every member of the commission considered himself a representative of the youth of the realm.

The commission members suggested several solutions of the youth problem.

One of the professors, a man who knew more about fish-grabbing-with-the-bare-hands than any other man in the paleolithic world, made a plea for the continued education of youth. "Let us put these young people back in school," he said. "Although they have studied elementary and advanced fish-grabbing, most of them have been very poorly taught. I get them in my freshmen classes in the university, and I know how ignorant they are. They have only the vaguest notions of how a fish should be grabbed with the bare hands. There is available in the journal and monograph literature of this subject a great mass of data which could be organized and taught to these young people in a good, stiff two- or three-year course on the junior college level, along with, possibly, some of the less important subjects. Thus when these

unemployed youths get old enough to acquire jobs
and family responsibilities, they will possess the
trained minds and hands which only the thorough
study of fish-grabbing can give them."

Professors of other subjects agreed with this
report in part, although they insisted that more
advanced courses in horse-clubbing and tiger-
scaring were even better designed than fish-grabbing to develop the strength and courage which
the young people would need so badly when and
if they finally got jobs.

The industrial leaders had a very different proposal. The fish chiefs' leading hired man suggested
that all workers over fifty years of age should be
retired and their places should be filled by young
men taken from the youth rock pile. "In the
fishing industry, for example," he explained,
"these older people now receive an average wage
of two fish per day. Although they get slower in
their work with advancing age, moreover, their
powerful and arrogant labor leaders threaten to
tie up the whole industry with a strike if we reduce
these wages. If they are retired under a tribal
pension scheme, the tribe can pay them an allow-

ance of one-half fish per day and the fishing industry can hire young people to replace them at one
fish per day. Thus unemployment will be mate-
rially reduced, the youth problem will be solved,
and the whole realm will benefit because the
fishing industry will be prosperous."

At this juncture the door of the conference room
was flung open and a small group of young men
and women burst into the room. After some argument their spokesman, a wild-eyed, hungry-look-
ing boy, was allowed to present the views of the
young people themselves.

"In spite of all the big piles of smoked fish, dried
meat, and tanned skins down there by the creek,"
he said, "there are many members of this tribe who
don't have enough to eat or wear. Our caves are
crowded, ugly, and insanitary. There is hardly
sleeping space in many of them; they are full of
bugs and lice and filth. We have no pictures on
the walls of our caves. We sit glumly by the fire
at night with never a song or a story to express our
emotions and lighten the dull load of living for
food and shelter alone. We need many things
which we do not now have and which we could

easily get if we were only permitted by the rules to work for them. We need more and better food, skins, shelter, songs, stories, and pictures.

"There is much work to be done, and we young people are ready and eager to do it. We can dig bigger and more convenient caves, we can learn how to cut down trees and make beautiful dwellings of wood such as the tribe over the mountains builds but which we have never enjoyed. We can make broad and smooth pathways back into the deep forest where other animals than antelopes live, and we can devise traps for those animals, thus improving and varying our food supply. We can compose songs and stories to delight the whole tribe. We can make pictures on the cave walls to show ourselves and the Great Mystery that we men are something more than the beasts who merely live, eat, drink, fight, reproduce their kind, and die. We are tired of playing with those damn' rocks up on the hill! Let us work, we beg of you wise old men, and we will increase the tribe's store of welfare and happiness more than enough to pay you for giving us this boon of labor."

The commission members were aghast at this radical proposal. They saw clearly that the poor boy who spoke did not understand the rules of the medicine men. They felt sorry about his ignorance and the ignorance of his little, misguided group of followers. But there was obviously only one thing to do, and so at a given signal from the presiding medicine man, the entire commission rose and with one accord threw the young people from the conference room. Then they sent an unofficial message to the Loyal Order of Stuffed-Horse Clubs, asking that the order should undertake immediately an investigation of un-paleolithic tendencies in the schools. As one of the medicine men said in an executive session of the commission, "We feel sure that these young people must have come under the tutelage of certain teachers who have thought about something more than educational matters of fish-grabbing, horse-clubbing, and tiger-scaring. A teacher who would do that is un-paleolithic to the core!"

After this disturbance was over, the commission settled down again to serious work and finally solved the youth problem. They organized a special administration to handle the problem. The administration sent out scouts to all the neighboring valleys and hills to search out new and bigger rock piles. As soon as discovery of a rock pile was made, experts were sent to classify and arrange the rocks for convenient play. Other experts were set to work devising rules for new games that could be played with rocks. Rock-play administrators and supervisors were appointed to organize and direct the work. A survey of all available youth was made with careful tabulation of individual and group preferences for big rocks and little rocks, gray rocks and red rocks, smooth rocks and rough rocks, round rocks and irregularly shaped rocks. Data were assembled and treated statistically, plans were drawn up, appropriations from the tribal fish and meat piles were made, and before long the greatest rock-pile movement in paleolithic history was well under way.

One day when the rock-pile players were busily engaged in their leisure-time activities under the direction of a corps of experts, a strange figure was seen to appear over the brow of the hill above the rock pile and watch the scene below him for a long time. At length one of the rock-pile supervisors became curious and climbed the slope to examine the stranger at close range.

"Greetings, friend," he called as he crawled over the last boulder that separated him from the solitary watcher.

The stranger raised his hand in the usual gesture of amity but said nothing. This taciturnity together with the fact that he was dressed in skins of an unfamiliar sort made him appear very foreign indeed. The rock-pile supervisor continued the friendly overture with some constraint in his manner. "I see you are watching our leisure-time program," he said politely, "and I wonder if I can help you in any way—give you information about our work—take you down to observe it in detail—anything—?"

"You call it a leisure-time program?" asked the stranger abruptly.

"Yes."

"What is leisure time?"

"Why—ah—it is the time you have when you don't have to work."

"Oh. I am looking for education. I thought this was some kind of an educational program."

"Well, in a way, it is."

"An educational program without work?"

"Yes."

"And with rocks?"

"Yes. They learn with rocks."

"*What* do they learn to do with rocks?"

"Well, they *play*—recreation, you know."

The stranger's eyes shifted ominously, and his hand tightened on the shaft of his hunting club. "They learn to *fight* with those rocks," he said flatly.

"Oh, no," protested the shocked supervisor, "not at all! Just recreation, I assure you."

"What's *recreation?*"

"Why—er—don't you *know?*"

"No."

"Don't you have a recreation program in your tribe?"

"No."

"Well, let me see, recreation is what you do to make a better life after you get through making a living."

"Oh. When do those young people down there work for a living?"

"Well, right now we have a lot of unemployment, you see, and these particular young people don't work. They have never worked."

"Never?"

"No, never. They have never had any jobs."

At this point the stranger showed clearly that he lacked manners. He stared hard at the rock-pile supervisor for much longer than the socially approved maximum. Then he turned without a word further and started back over the brow of the hill toward the hinterland whence he had come.

"A good journey to you!" the supervisor called in courteous farewell.

The stranger nodded grimly over his shoulder, struck a smart blow with his hunting club at a wayside boulder, and then dropped out of sight down the trail.

VII · THE DISINTEGRATION OF DR. PEDDIWELL

IT WAS a gray morning for Tijuana, and the professor appeared distrait. The comic mirrors along the wall might as well have been nonexistent for all the attention he gave them. The long stretch of bar appeared no longer to have philosophical meaning for him. He slumped in his chair at the table and toyed apathetically with his daisy glass. I tried one line of attack after another in a vain effort to find the adequate stimulus for a lecture, but finally I fell silent too. It must have been that a premonition of disaster was slowing my cerebral processes. I know that something gave my daisy a faint bouquet of castor oil. That must have been a subjective phenomenon, for Luis was a most careful bartender.

At last the professor himself broke the ice. "Do you know what lecture this is?" he asked dully.

"What lecture?" I repeated, stupid with surprise.

"It is the *sixth* lecture, the *last* lecture, in fact it is the lecture after the lecture that *should* have been the last lecture."

"Sixth? *Should* have been last?"

"You remember I had only five days to spend on this course? The time is up. It was really up yesterday. I gave myself one day extra, but now the absolute deadline approaches."

Now I knew the reason for Dr. Peddiwell's strange manner. I had lost track of the days, of course, but his keen time sense had checked them off like a navigator's chronometer.

"Do you *have* to leave today, Doctor?" I asked miserably.

"Yes," said the great man resolutely. "I have to go—tonight. Tomorrow morning, according to the itinerary carefully arranged for me by Mrs. Peddiwell who attends faithfully to the details of all my journeys lest I get disconcerted by the way, I must appear in San Diego fresh from my scholarly labors in the north—er—was it Palo Alto, Stanford, where I have been working?"

"No, sir. Berkeley. At least you told me that you were working in the library this week at the University of California."

"Quite right, sir. And that is where it was, or rather where *I* was, or am, until tonight when I shall take a train south and arrive at San Diego in the morning to greet the little woman and escort her back to Petaluma. The final sessions of the League of American Needlewomen will be—er—pulled off, I think the phrase is, tonight in a blaze of oratory, and Mrs. Peddiwell must hasten to retail to the Petaluma chapter of the organization all those lessons she has learned at the national convention while they are still fresh in her memory."

"Ah, well," I said consolingly, pretending to a courage I did not feel. "There will be other times. We'll come back to Tijuana again. Once more you will lecture before this longest of all long bars in the world. Once more we shall—"

"No," interrupted the professor firmly. "It is not to be."

"But surely you can—surely Mrs. Peddiwell will permit you to arrange—surely she will attend another convention some—"

"Oh, yes, no doubt." He brushed the question of his wife's future whereabouts to one side as though it were of less than no consequence to him. "But that is not the prime issue. The prime issue is this." He lowered his voice almost to a conspiratorial whisper. *"Today's lecture is really the last one because it deals with the last of the mate,ial."*

"You mean—?"

"I mean I am at the end of my knowledge of the paleolithic field. Beyond this point my researches do not go. I have tried this morning, but after I go a little ways I come to a veil which I cannot penetrate. Perhaps another scholar—more gifted—more industrious—more sensitive to daisies—might hope to go somewhat further—but for me, it is finished!"

His manner was so sure, so impressive in its humility, that I could not say a word. I merely sat in silence and waited for the summarizing statement which I hoped would come.

I have tried to see what was happening in the valley of the tribe on the other side of the mountain (Dr. Peddiwell began hesitantly), the tribe to which the strange observer of rock-pile recreation belonged, but it has been hard to get very much. I have had some success, it is true, but the details are not very clear. The general import is unmistakable, however.

This strange tribe had a single ruler. He was a practical man who had little interest in magic or culture. His shoulders bulged with hard muscles as he swung his heavy club. His brow was lined with the deep marks of an habitually fierce scowl. His massive chin jutted aggressively at any men or events that attempted to stand even momentarily against his will. When he spoke, he always shouted in rhythmic, guttural grunt-patterns which had powerful hypnotic effects on his people. Under the stimulus of his grunts and example, they too shouted rhythmically, waved their clubs fiercely, and stamped in unison until the ground trembled beneath their heavy tread.

The ultramontane tribe was not troubled with unemployment. All the men and boys who could possibly be spared from hunting and fishing were put to work for the tribe by the ruler. They gathered rocks as did the recreation group on the other side of the hill, but instead of playing with the rocks they made weapons of them. Some stones they selected for hand missiles, others they put aside for use in slings, and still others they shaped into axes which they bound to stout handles.

Only half of the working day of this group was spent in making weapons, however. The remaining daylight hours were devoted to practice in the use of these weapons. The first result of this specialization in weapons was a very effective system of hunting. Fewer and fewer men were needed to supply the tribe with food and clothing, and more and more men could be assigned to the tasks of making and learning to use weapons. The second result was that as the members of the tribe developed skill in the use of weapons they developed also an intense and growing desire to employ the weapons in war against some other tribe.

The scowling ruler talked of various reasons why the tribe might well go to war. He spoke of tribal destiny, of tribal honor, and of tribal need for achievement of bloody ends, but most of all he spoke of inferior peoples who must have their ways changed with clubs. The real reason that he and the tribe desired war, however, was to use their weapons and to secure a wealth of meat and skins by fighting rather than by work of a more prosaic kind. Like other men, they did not commonly speak of their real reason for the action they were going to follow.

The tribe had really reached a peak in potential fighting skill. The ruler recognized that fact and was beginning to be worried about it. He knew that there was danger of overtraining his men if he drilled them much longer without having them fight somebody. He could not continue to scowl and grunt forever about future military glories; he had to have an actual battle or two to talk about. Moreover, he was getting a little weary of his own speeches. He yearned for action so intensely that his clubbing muscles ached.

The ruler was delighted, therefore, when his comparative-education scout returned and reported the state of affairs in the community over the mountain.

"But don't those people have rocks?" the ruler asked.

"Oh, yes, Your Bigness," answered the scout, "but they do not really use them—at least not for any purpose of importance."

"Don't use them! What the hell do you mean?"

"Well, they monkey with the rocks in various ways, but they don't do anything with them for the good of the tribe."

"But how can they get the tribe's work done that way? Are you trying to be funny with me, you crawling worm?"

"No, no, Great One. I have never a thought for anything but the sober truth. I know that what I say sounds unbelievable, but I am giving you as true a picture as I know how to give. Those people over there don't have any notion of what they want the tribe to become."

"Don't they have any education to give them a notion?"

"No, Bigness, not in the sense of an activity planned to put the tribe nearer to any clear-cut goal. They do have something they *call* education, but it is just a collection of traditional activities, a machine which they worship for its own sake. The result is pitiful. They have plenty of meat to eat and skins to wear, but they are so uneducated that they don't know how to distribute food and covering, and consequently many of them are wretchedly fed and clothed. They have a tremendous amount of work to do, yet they are so uneducated that they force many of their people to be idle all the time. They are forever blocked in attempts to better their lives by reason of having only mis-education, pseudo education, in place of real education."

The great ruler's scowl deepened. "Good," he muttered. "Such a people need to be taken over by a superior race. We march at dawn. See that the necessary orders are given now."

Dr. Peddiwell fell into silence again. I waited for him to go on with the story, but he continued to stare moodily at his glass without a word.

"And *did* they march?" I finally ventured.

"They did," he answered shortly.

"And how did the war come out?" I persisted.

"What would you think?" asked the professor. "I have given you the background. I have told you how New-Fist's tribe started with a system of purposeful education and how that education was degenerated through the years into a system of red-tape, magical culture. Use your imagination, my friend. I have used mine until it is exhausted. I have to start for San Diego."

"*Start for San Diego*," repeated a voice so grim that it could hardly be called feminine though it came undoubtedly from some kind of a woman. The professor whirled in his chair as though in response to the crack of a rifle and then slumped back as though the bullet had hit him between the eyes. I looked up and remained frozen by what I saw standing behind him.

In the ten years since I had seen her, Mrs. Peddiwell had grown somewhat grayer, somewhat broader, but her characteristic unpleasantness of manner had not changed a whit so far as I could judge.

"Start for San Diego?" she repeated harshly, stepping forward in order to glare down more readily at her husband's stricken countenance "And why, rnay I ask, J. Abner Peddiwell, do you happen to be starting from *here?*"

The professor did not attempt to answer, and probably his wife did not expect him to answer, for she went on swiftly in the same merciless tone. "Here in a *saloon!* With a dirty bum!" She eyed me momentarily, but with obvious disfavor. "And what's this? Are you *drinking?* Have you actually been drinking *liquor?*" She snatched up his half-filled daisy glass, held it briefly to her nostrils, and then smashed it viciously on the table top. The crash brought both of us automatically to our feet.

Luis dashed through a bar portal and came running forward with a towel and an agonized expression. Dr. Peddiwell handed him a twenty-peso note and spoke in brief farewell. "Good-by, Luis," he murmured quietly. "I am going away. No more daisies, Luis, ever."

"You weel come back, Senor," Luis assured him sympathetically. Before the professor could answer, his wife had caught his arm in a powerful grip and was propelling him rapidly toward the door.

I am proud of what I did then. Although the mere sight of that woman paralyzed me, I fought off my terror and rushed forward to grasp the professor's free hand. "Thank you for the lectures, Doctor," I said chokingly. "I can never repay you!"

"Don't mention it, my friend," he replied politely. No circumstance, however terrifying, could take from him his sure sense of proper courtesy. Then, with a faint smile as he was being dragged through the door, he added, "*But my chronology must have been off by one day!*"

Catalog

If you are interested in a list of fine Paperback
books, covering a wide range of subjects
and interests, send your name and address,
requesting your free catalog, to:

McGraw-Hill Paperbacks
11 West 19th Street
New York, N.Y. 10011